ROCKET-POWERED SCIENCE

Invent to Learn!

Create, Build & Test Rocket Designs

Ed Sobey

A GOOD YEAR BOOK™

02/08
14.95

Dedicated to

Woody and Andrew

Who launched water rockets with me

On hot summer days

Good Year Books

Are available for most basic curriculum subjects plus many enrichment areas. For more Good Year Books, contact your local bookseller or educational dealer. For a complete catalog with information about other Good Year Books, please contact:

Good Year Books
P.O. Box 91858
Tucson, AZ 85752-1858
www.goodyearbooks.com

Cover design: Gary Smith, Performance Design
Text design: Doug Goewey

ISBN-10: 1-59647-055-0
ISBN-13: 978-1-59647-055-2
1 2 3 4 5 6 7 8 9 10 – MZ – 08 07 06 05

Contents

1 *Blasting Off with Rockets, Jets, and Ballistics* 9

Demonstration

2 *Powered by Balloons* 15

Demonstrations

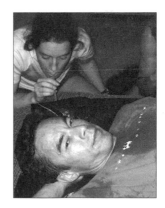

Models to Make

Preface

The irony of teaching rocket science to rocket scientists hit me during a presentation at NASA Langley Research Center. The scientists and engineers had invited me (not a rocket scientist) to help them with the outreach programs that they present to public schools. To introduce them to using hands-on activities, I had them making paper rockets and testing them. As you might expect, the rocket scientists had a great time making rockets. What you might not expect happened, too: They learned.

With the activities in *Rocket-powered Science*, kids have the same two experiences: They learn and they want to keep making and testing rockets. Doing science, any kind of science, beats reading about or hearing about science every time. Kids think, work hard, and learn when they do science. "Doing science" means asking questions and conducting experiments to answer them. Kids naturally learn this way.

Both professional rocket scientists and elementary students can learn from participating in the activities described in *Rocket-powered Science*. Both will have fun and won't want to quit. The trick to doing this is to convince the kids that they are rocket scientists and to convince the rocket scientists that they are kids.

Have a blast!

—Ed Sobey

About the Author

Ed Sobey has written sixteen books, most of which are on inventing and science, and has hosted two television series. After earning his Ph.D. in physical oceanography from Oregon State University, Ed worked as a polar oceanographer, assessing the impacts of oil spills in the Arctic and sub-Arctic. He spent a winter in Antarctica, has participated in two dozen ocean research expeditions, and has sailed across the Pacific Ocean in a sailboat. Ed is a Fellow of The Explorers Clubs and chairs the Pacific Northwest Chapter.

Leaving research, Ed joined the South Florida Science Museum and started a new career as a museum director. He has directed five museums and was founding director of the National Inventors Hall of Fame and founder of the National Toy Hall of Fame. He was elected president of the Ohio Museums Association and taught museum management at the University of Washington.

In 1999, Ed started the Northwest Invention Center, which provides traveling exhibits and educational workshops for museums in Europe, Asia, and North America. The Center also works in conjunction with Kids Invent! to develop new inventing-based learning programs for kids. Between professional activities Ed runs, bikes, swims, SCUBA dives, and kayaks.

Getting Started

On the Launch Pad

When you tell students that they are going to make and launch rockets, you fire their interest and focus their attention. Doing "rocket science" is as cool as science gets. Even cooler is that they get to design and build the rockets themselves. They don't follow a cookbook or pattern; they're free to express their ideas. They become rocket scientists.

You can build on the excitement and foster the interest by following our methods of "inventing to learn." Even without the methodology, these rocket activities will provide fun learning experiences. With the methodology, you will establish new levels of learning interest.

The allure of rocket science (and inventing and other sciences) is coming up with new ideas, testing them, and seeing the product of your creativity fly high. It's what fuels the excitement at NASA, and it can fuel the excitement at your school or home school. Remove the elements of self-discovery and innovation and you lessen the interest and lose much of the learning value. So, instead of teaching a unit on rocket science, create a NASA-like design laboratory. Instead of talking about rocket science, establish a team of rocket scientists and engineers who pursue their own research interests.

Your Role as Head Rocket Scientist

In *Rocket-powered Science*, the doing of science is divided into activities that lend themselves to demonstrations of phenomena ("Try This") and those that encourage experimentation ("Models to Make"). It also provides historical context for the technology being discussed ("Rocket-powered History") and examples of how the technology demonstrated is applied ("Rocket-powered Applications").

This book assumes that you, the teacher or presenter, will be conducting the demonstrations. However, students can also present them. Anyone doing a demonstration should wear safety goggles to model safety procedures.

Like the demonstrations, the models in this book are directed at an adult demonstrating to students. The models include building and testing activities, some of which encourage measurement, collection, and analysis of data. Some also encourage additional experimentation.

Your role in the lab is to provide the challenges (the tasks to be accomplished and the goals against which each will be measured) and materials, and to launch teams into higher orbits of understanding. The instructions for each demonstration and model in this book outline the challenges and list the materials you will need. Many are recycled materials that you can gather for free. The rest are inexpensive. That leaves the question of how to launch teams into higher orbits.

To get outer-space results in the classroom, treat your students as NASA engineers. Challenge them to work in teams to solve design problems that you issue. Tell them the criteria they will use to measure success and show them the materials they can use. Then, get out of their way.

Once you've issued a challenge, let teams work with a minimum of guidance. Let them make mistakes or head directly toward success without criticism. As long as they are working diligently, they are learning. Encourage them and push them to make prototypes quickly, but otherwise let them work on their own.

Design Philosophy

When doing something new, it's almost always better to speed through design and start making and testing prototypes quickly rather than overanalyzing what you don't know. Schools have taught students to spend time designing and thinking instead of prototyping, and you'll have to overcome this tendency. Not that we're against thinking. Quite the contrary, we're advocating thinking with brains and hands. Unless you have experience in designing rockets, you won't be able to foresee the design difficulties until you assemble the components and test them. So get on with it and understand that you're going to make mistakes.

We tell rocket scientists to work quickly and make mistakes as quickly as possible. Because they won't know if they're making mistakes until they test prototypes, they have to make their prototypes quickly.

In designing their rockets some kids will want to sketch designs, others will talk to each other, and others will want to build immediately. All are methods of thinking. Kids express their preferred learning styles by how they undertake the design process. In learning to invent methodology, kids are free to work and think in their own ways.

Although some students will avoid making sketch designs before they build (preferring to design in three dimensions either in their minds or with their hands), they do need the experience of expressing ideas on paper. You can have them document their designs with drawings and text as part of a culminating project.

As teams work on their challenges, your job as the Design Chief is to circulate among them and check progress. You should not tell teams how they are doing or how they should be tackling the problem, but you should ask how they are doing and how

Rocket-powered History:

The Rockets' Red Glare

During the War of 1812, British troops fired Congreve rockets at Fort McHenry in Maryland. These rockets were made before the invention of fins and used a 16-foot-long staff to guide them. Sir William Congreve developed the rockets and the British used them during the Napoleonic Wars, as well as the War of 1812. The rockets could travel as far as 1.5 miles (2.4 kilometers). Francis Scott Key, who witnessed the attack, wrote the "Star-Spangled Banner" based on the battle.

they are tackling the problem. When kids answer your questions, they have to think about what they are doing and have to express their ideas in words. The expression of ideas in words is a vital thinking process that they may avoid unless you ask them questions. Asking questions also allows them to express their existing knowledge base, showing you their level of understanding or misunderstanding.

When you see an obvious mistake—kids showing a naive misunderstanding of science—encourage them to test their ideas, and make sure you are present when they do. Faced with research results that contradict preconceived understandings, most people attribute the failings to conditions and not to their understanding. Your job at this stage is to ensure that they confront their misunderstandings and not intellectually duck out of learning. Ask them questions about what happened and why it happened. Force them to test each hypothesis they toss out as to the origin of the outcomes until they see that they need a new understanding. You can assist them by asking questions and ensuring intellectual honesty.

A case in point is making a car or boat powered by a balloon. It is common among kids (and adults) to mount a sail on the vehicle for the balloon (also mounted on the vehicle) to blow on. The thinking is that the balloon needs a surface to blow against to propel the boat or car. Of course, jets and rockets don't carry sails behind their engines, and they wouldn't work if they did. But, explaining that to kids without giving them the opportunity to test their ideas gives rise to two sets of understanding: one to use in the classroom and one to apply in the real world. Forcing the confrontation of ideas is the only way for them to consolidate their understandings. Allowing, even encouraging, balloon sail models consolidates understanding through failure and analysis of the failure.

We point out where students often make mistakes and give suggestions for where to tie in standards-based content in the boxes called "Learning Moments." These are valuable opportunities for you to help students make connections between their experiences and a firmer understanding of the science involved.

A Discussion of Failure

Failure, as Thomas Edison proclaimed, is a stepping stone to understanding. Unlike most learning activities, inventing to learn encourages thoughtful mistakes as a method of learning. In fact, it encourages making mistakes as quickly as possible as the fastest way of learning.

Accepting and even encouraging failures gives students freedom to try even their "dumb" ideas. Everyone will encourage students to test their great ideas—there is no freedom there. Allowing them to test what may appear to be dumb or what they're not confident of is granting freedom to experiment. A very few of these ideas will lead directly to success, but most will not. However, nearly all will lead to better understanding and to satiating one bit of curiosity.

Teams will work long and hard as long as you give them the freedom to make mistakes and have successes of their own design. The first design undoubtedly won't work well. New designs rarely do. It takes engineering and experimentation to find the optimal designs. This is an iterative process, like practicing hitting a ball. Each swing provides information on how to refine the swing for better results. By working fast, teams will have opportunities for many tests of their designs and will have a much better chance of meeting the design goals.

The Inventing to Learn Model

Of utmost importance is helping students observe, report, and relate the results of experiments. They aren't practiced at watching something happen and giving an accurate report of what they saw. Asking a student what his or her rocket did during a test flight will evoke responses such as "I wasn't watching," "I'm not good at science," or "It needs bigger fins." Instead of reporting what they saw, they will avoid the possibility of being wrong by giving a nonresponsive answer. Insist that they report to you what happened and if they can't, have them repeat the experiment with the understanding that you'll ask the same question again.

Once students observe and report the qualitative results of their experiments, challenge them to relate the observed results to a design feature of their rocket. If the rocket tumbled in flight, what feature of the rocket allowed it (or caused it) to tumble? Once these two questions ("What did the rocket do?" and "What caused it to do that?") are answered, they can propose a single design change to test in the next experiment.

Most students (and many adults) are not disciplined to address these questions. Because science can't be done unless the practitioners can report accurately what occurred and understand that there has to be a cause for the results, developing these skills is your primary responsibility in teaching science. To meet this responsibility, station yourself at the testing area and engage each student or team of students after each experiment.

After getting students to observe and report, and to associate what they saw to elements of the model they've created, the next most important task is to get them to figure out which one design element they should change before testing again. Some teams will want to keep testing the same rocket without making change. This adds little to the knowledge base and should be discouraged. Some will want to make several changes at once. If they do, they won't know which of the changes they made led to the improvement they observe in the next test. Insist on changing one, and only one, variable between each launch.

After each test, also ask them how the results compare to their most recent test. Did the rocket go farther or not as far? Then ask them what change they made between experiments. (They should have made only one change so they can assess its impact on the rocket's flight.) If the change made a big improvement in the distance traveled, should they continue to make the same type of change again? If not, what other design feature should they alter to improve their rocket? Your questions will help stimulate thinking and team dialogue.

Here are other elements of the "inventing to learn model":

• Provide a clear and measurable goal for each activity. When students measure their own results, the results inherently improve. Make sure they know what the goals are and have them record their team achievements prominently on the board. Students should make and record the measurements themselves. In most cases the activities require measuring distances, which are easily done with yard- or meter sticks or measuring tapes. Students need experience making and recording measurements and graphing and analyzing them. These skills are included in the mathematics standards and are an important learning experience.

• Design the activity so it provides immediate feedback on how their model is working. That is, they shouldn't have to ask how they are doing; they will see the results themselves. Having immediate and apparent feedback is critical to keeping people engaged in a repetitive task. Imagine hitting golf balls at a driving range, but rather than seeing (and feeling) how well you hit each ball, you had to wait six weeks for a report card. You would quickly grow bored with hitting balls. If students know what the goals are and are charged with making the measurements themselves, they will have the immediate feedback required to motivate them.

• Encourage higher levels of success. Schools teach kids to do a task once and turn it in. In engineering, science, and most of life, you keep improving your initial products based on information you learn through testing. Kids are programmed to quit testing after one or two successes. Your job is to set the bar for success ever higher and to keep them improving and testing their models. If their rocket traveled 99 feet (30 meters), can they improve it to go at least 100 feet (30.5 meters)? Can it break the existing school record? Because each refinement in design provides an opportunity for refining understanding, you have to press them to continue to improve.

• As teams make learning discoveries, help them solidify their understanding by giving them the appropriate vocabulary that describes what they experienced, relating the science concepts, and giving them examples of how the same effect is manifested in other situations. For example, as teams work on improving the flight of their rockets, you can point out that those things they added to the fuselage are called fins. Fins are there to control the direction of flight, not to provide lift (as wings on airplanes do). You can ask questions that direct their thinking to issues of energy transfer (what is the source of the energy that propelled the rocket; where did the energy of motion go?), motion, and forces.

• Use culminating activities to draw together their understanding and express it in different intelligence modes. Verbalizing their experience will give them a second level of understanding, in addition to the physical experience of making and testing the models. Having them sketch their rocket and label the components adds a third level of understanding. As kids express their understanding in different intelligence modes, they improve their understanding and reinforce the learning.

• Evaluate each student's success of learning through the culminating activities or reports that they prepare. Challenge them to find real-world applications of the phenomena they witnessed and imagine new applications. To wrap in historical threads, have them use the Internet to search for the inventors or discoverers associated with the activity. They can also search for information on how rockets, jets, and other engines or vehicles work to add to their reports.

• Challenge them to continue. These activities are so engaging that kids (and siblings, parents, and friends) will continue them at home, if you provide encouragement. Tell them where they can get the components and challenge them to beat the class records. Have them bring in their best designs to share with the class. Your encouragement can transform a one- or two-hour classroom activity into an evening's fun learning for a family, easily doubling or tripling the time spent in each activity.

Rocket-powered History:

The First Satellite

The first satellite was launched atop a three-stage Russian rocket in 1957. The launch of *Sputnik I* opened the space age and great concern about the United States' scientific and technology capabilities. Three and a half months after *Sputnik* entered outer space, the United States launched its first satellite, *Explorer I*.

Competition

Throughout these activities students will express competitive spirits, and these help fan the flames of innovation and energize everyone. We have teams write their team name (not their real names) on the board and list the distances their rocket travels. This visible display of data provokes diligent work on everyone's part.

Rather than a true competition in which there is but one winner and many losers, kids create their own categories of excellence that they celebrate: "Even if your rocket went farther, mine looked neater." To encourage the sense that all who experiment and innovate win, celebrate the creative designs as well as the designs that excelled in meeting the stated goals. When holding class discussions, don't talk about "Johnny's rocket" and how well it did, focus on the features of the rocket that went farthest: "Look at the symmetric and neat fins on this rocket." Focus praise and criticism on the design elements and not on the individuals.

Following this pedagogic style will change the classroom atmosphere into a high-energy chaos where ideas, design, thinking, and teamwork are valued. Kids will learn from the experiments they run and from each other, and, secondarily, from you. Instead of focusing on your presentation (and on maintaining good behavior), you can focus on teaching one-on-one at the optimal learning moments. You will have time to anticipate problems and attend to them because students are actively engaged in activities they enjoy. The very rare behavioral issues are handled by suggesting that the offending student be denied the opportunity to build and test his or her rocket. Thus, rather than being in a position of forcing kids to do science, this approach puts you in the position in which the threat of not being able to do science will control behavior.

Rocket-propelled Science Standards

So, why launch into rocket science? Because it propels kids into learning that is directly tied to the state science (or math or technology) standards and gets them doing science, rather than merely reading about science. It is a more effective approach to learning and one that kids enjoy.

In making and testing these models, students will learn nearly all of the physical science content and will experience science inquiry firsthand. Specifically, each activity should include:

1. Making a model. Designing it, either on paper and then building it, or building it and later sketching the two-dimensional design—most kids will want to start building as soon as they get their hands on materials. If time is short, this is the best approach. However, by having each team make a design sketch, you ensure that they at least talk to one another and agree on the design before they start to build. Also, the thought processes involved in two-dimensional and three-dimensional design are different, and these activities provide a good exercise in thinking using both processes.

2. Testing the model. Rockets need to be tested, not once, or twice, but many times. It is in the testing and analysis that most learning occurs. Science and engineering are iterative processes, where each inquiry or attempt yields a piece of information that moves the team toward better understanding and success in meeting the challenge. Ensure that they change one variable for each test and that they record what they changed and the impact it had (how far their rocket went).

3. Measuring. You will be surprised by the difficulty that some students will have measuring a rocket's position. Operating a yard- or meter stick is much more difficult than talking about how to operate it, and these activities beg for students to do real measurement. Even if they can pass a test on measurement, they will learn a lot by making measurements in the field.

4. Data recording. Provide data logs or have them record data on the board. Remind them that the purpose of recording data is to learn so they can improve their rocket. This requires that they record what change they made and what impact it had, along with the raw distance measurement. When they need information that they forgot to record, point out how easy it would have been had they recorded it rather than having to repeat an experiment.

5. Graphing. Several of the activities provide data that can be graphed. Students need help preparing graphs and interpreting them. Have them graph data such as the angle of launch vs. the distance the rocket flew, or the launch air pressure vs. time aloft. Have them prepare neat graphs showing the actual data points, with lightly drawn lines connecting the data points. Graphs need labels explaining what the graph represents, what variables are drawn along each axis, and what units are used. With completed graph in hand, have each student describe to you what the graph represents while pointing to what they are describing.

6. Reporting. Having students write up a report on their project strengthens their understanding. Having to commit their ideas in writing connects understanding and ties different modes of thinking together. Verbal reporting is good too, but often students slip by with sloppy thinking. Writing—on paper or as a Web page with photographs—is a great way to culminate a project and evaluate understanding.

7. Content. Every state has its own way of specifying the content it expects students to learn. Having students treat each activity as a science experiment will take them through the "Science as Inquiry" standards and "The Nature of Science"

standards. You will find that the activities in this book cover the vast majority of the content standards listed under physical sciences. Here is a listing of typical standards met by the activities in this book:

- Properties of objects and materials

- Positions and motions of objects

- Motions and forces (including friction)

- Sound

- Transfer of energy: storage of energy, potential and kinetic energy, heat; physical and chemical reactions

- Technology design: systems and designs

- Science as a human endeavor: history of science and technology

- Mathematics: computation, measurement, data collecting and graphing

- Communication of results

- Critical-thinking skills

You may find other areas of content embedded in these activities, but clearly there are enough to warrant expending the effort to gather materials and prepare for hands-on learning. If you have any doubts, watch your students after you give them the challenge of making a rocket fly far.

IMPORTANT SAFETY NOTE

For all demonstrations and team activities that involve rockets and propelled objects, make sure that everyone—you included—is wearing eye protection.

Chapter 1

Blasting Off With Rockets, Jets, and Ballistics

Rockets move forward by burning fuels and venting them in the direction opposite to the desired travel. As the fuel burns in the combustion chamber, it generates hot gases that expand and push out the exhaust nozzle. The gases escaping to the rear force the rocket forward. This simple system provides more power than any other engine of comparable size.

Rockets are one type of jet propulsion. Jet engines in airplanes are another. In general, rockets carry their own supply of oxygen to mix with fuel so they can operate outside the earth's atmosphere. Jets and missiles operate in the earth's atmosphere and draw air into combustion chambers, where the air is mixed with fuel and burns. Aside from this difference, jet engines and rocket engines operate similarly.

A liquid-fuel rocket engine heats gases to about 5,000 degrees Fahrenheit (°F), or 2,760 degrees Centigrade (°C). This causes the gas molecules to move about three times faster than they do at room temperatures. The engine converts chemical energy stored in the fuel to kinetic energy of the moving molecules. The faster-moving molecules raise the pressure inside the combustion chamber and move toward the area of lower pressure outside the nozzle.

Note that the high temperatures of rocket exhaust gases are hot enough to melt many of the materials we commonly use. Even much cooler jet airplane exhaust reaches 3,600°F, which is hot enough to melt the aluminum that the engine is made of. Obviously, operating at these high temperatures requires development of new materials and creative engineering.

The nozzle directs the exhaust to extract the most energy possible from the gases. It only allows gas to escape in the direction that is opposite to the direction of the rocket's motion. The shape of the nozzle speeds up the exhaust and causes the pressure to drop, which transfers more thrust to the rocket. (Louis Bloomfield's book, *How Things Work: The Physics of Everyday Life*, has a nice section explaining how nozzles work.)

continued on next page ➤

A common misconnection is that these exhaust gases have to push against something to give thrust to the rocket. A physics student observed that aircraft carriers raise panels on the deck behind planes taking off to give the exhaust better leverage. (The raised panels are there to protect the people and equipment on the deck.) If this were true, rockets couldn't operate in the void of space where there is nothing to push against. It is the downward acceleration of the gases that has an equal and opposite reaction that pushes the rocket upward. The gases don't have to push on the ground to lift the rocket.

Similarly, in airplanes and helicopters the wings (or rotors) deflect air downward. Thus the wings exert a force on the air, so the air exerts an equal and opposite force on the wings. This force is the lift that keeps aircraft in the air. The downward-moving air doesn't have to press against the ground to provide lift; it provides lift because the wing deflects it downward. (If it were true that the downward-moving air has to push against the ground to provide lift, helicopters would have difficulty as they climb farther away from the ground. The upper limitation on flight is not the distance from the ground, but the density of air that the rotors deflect downward and that the engines need to mix with fuel.)

Try This:
Soda Can Engine

Here is an easy way to visualize how rockets and jets propel themselves in one direction by forcing out fluid in the opposite direction. The force powering this engine is gravity.

Materials

- Empty aluminum soda can
- String
- Nails

Procedure

1. Tie one end of the string to the tab opener on the top of the can. You can use this to suspend the can. You'll get even better results from this experiment if you tie the upper end of the string to a fishing swivel (available at sporting goods stores) to allow the string to turn without twisting.

2. Poke two holes on opposite sides of the can as close to the bottom as possible. Cover the holes with your fingers and fill the can with water. When the can is full, let the water flow out of the holes as you support the can only by the string. In a few seconds the water will have drained out of the can without imparting any significant motion to the can.

3. Insert the nail back in each of the holes and bend it parallel to the base of the can toward the left. Repeat the experiment to see water flowing out of the can toward the left side of both holes and to see the can spinning toward the right.

Explanation

By bending the nozzles (openings in the can), you created an engine. The can now exerts a force on the water to get it to flow toward the left. The water exerts an equal and opposite force on the can, pushing it toward the right.

You can repeat the experiment by making more holes or making holes with different-sized nails. Dry off the can and cover the first set of holes with masking tape. Then make a new set. See what arrangement and size of holes causes the most revolutions of the can.

Model rockets are propelled the same way large rockets are. An engine containing fuel is inserted into a hollow cylinder, often a cardboard tube. The rocketeer closes a switch that passes electrical current to a small igniter at the base of the engine.

continued on next page ➤

Soda Can Engine (continued)

The current heats the igniter and that causes the engine to burn. The engine generates hot gases from combustion, and these escaping gases lift the rocket. A launch rod guides the rocket upward, and once in the air and moving fast, fins located on the base of the cylinder guide the rocket.

Fourth of July fireworks rockets work the same way. A fuse ignites coarsely ground gunpowder, and as it burns, it generates hot gases that exhaust through an opening in the bottom. These fast-moving exhaust gases push the rocket in the opposite direction.

Rockets that explode or send off second stages have additional charges of gunpowder. To get gunpowder to explode, rather than ignite and burn, it is ground to a finer power, which increases the surface area available for igniting.

Rockets or missiles originally had wooden tails to provide stability. The Chinese are credited with inventing rockets around AD 1200. Their fuel was a combination of sulfur, charcoal, and saltpeter (potassium nitrate). This fuel, packed into a hollowed-out piece of bamboo, would launch skyward when ignited.

These first rockets used a guide stick to keep them traveling in the desired direction. English inventor William Hale exchanged three fins for the guide stick in the mid-1800s. This innovation greatly improved the accuracy of the rockets.

Rockets without guide sticks or fins tend to tumble in flight. As they fly, any disturbance in the flow of air past the rocket exerts a force on the rocket. The force can cause the rocket to turn away from its line of flight, and without stabilizing fins, it will continue to turn and tumble. Once it tumbles, it presents a much larger surface area for air molecules to have an impact and it quickly loses speed and falls to the ground.

Rocket-powered History:

The First Engine

Hero of Alexandria invented a steam engine around AD 60. His engine used steam to spin a sphere. A fire heated water that turned into steam and flowed into the sphere, which was free to turn. He vented the steam from the sphere through two pipes, and the escaping steam turned the sphere. The soda can engine models Hero's engine; however, it uses water and gravity instead of expanding gases to propel it.

To get a rocket to fly well, it needs to have some drag behind the center of mass. Fins near the base of a rocket provide drag that returns the rocket to its path.

Students (and adults, too) confuse fins with wings. Fins provide drag. Yes, drag slows the rocket down, but the drag provides control to keep the back of the rocket from racing in front of the front of the rocket (tumbling). Airplanes have wings to provide lift; of course, they also provide drag, but drag is the price you pay for getting lift. Rockets don't need lift; they use their energy to overcome the pull of gravity. Like bullets and artillery shells, rockets don't fly per se (don't require lift), but they punch through the air as ballistic projectiles.

When students build rocket models with wings (instead of fins), the results are usually disappointing. Their rockets have high drag, travel slowly, and may glide, but they don't (typically) travel far. To work effectively, fins need to be placed at the rear of the rocket and need to be as small as possible (minimizing the drag) while being large enough to stabilize the flight.

With this introduction, let us make a distinction between the different models that follow in this book. Most models are not true rockets: You'll be delighted to know that you won't have 5,000-degree blasts of exhaust gases blowing through your classroom. Two of the models use chemical reactions to generate higher-pressure gases that propel the rockets. Several of the models look like rockets and fly like rockets but are propelled with an initial launch force. Straw rockets and pneumatic blast rockets are examples. Some use jet engines (venting high pressure fluids in the direction opposite to the flight); the water rocket is one. Regardless of whether each model meets the specific criteria of a rocket, students will learn science in these demonstrations and activities.

Rocket-powered History:

Faster Than Sound

Chuck Yeager was the first person to fly a plane faster than the speed of sound, in 1947. He flew a rocket-powered plane, the X-1.

Chapter 2

Powered by Balloons

Blowing up a balloon allows you to store energy. Inside an inflated balloon the molecules of air are pushed closer together than they are outside the balloon. The pressure is higher inside, and when we release the air, there are several ways we can apply this stored energy. But before we let the air out of the bag, let's figure out what's keeping it in.

Rocket-powered History:

The First Balloons

The first balloon was made by one of the world's greatest scientists, Michael Faraday, in 1824. Probably not in a party mood, he needed a way to collect gases he generated in experiments. He cut out two circles of rubber and pressed their edges together to form a seal. To keep the rest of the two pieces of rubber from sticking together, he sprinkled flour between them. The edges held, and he was able to inflate the balloons. Faraday was one of the greatest scientists of all time, making discoveries in electricity, magnetism, and chemistry, as well as inventing balloons.

The first toy balloons came as a kit for the buyer to assemble. The modern balloon, made of Vulcanized rubber, was first sold in England in 1847. It was Charles Goodyear's discovery of Vulcanization three years earlier that allowed rubber to be improved and used in balloons and many other products. Vulcanization is the process of heating and adding sulfur to rubber that gives rubber its strength and enduring elasticity.

A Note On:

Latex Balloons

Most balloons that you purchase at a party store are made of latex rubber. They are made by dipping forms into vats of latex, which comes from the sap of rubber trees. The latex stops air from escaping from a balloon or greatly slows down the flow. As more air is forced into the balloon, the latex stretches and exerts its elastic force on the air inside. Here are some things to try when exploring balloons.

Try This:
Blow Up a Balloon

Materials

• Latex balloons, 10 to 12 inches long

Procedure

1. Grab a balloon at each end and tug on it. It acts like a rubber band and resists being stretched. It also resists being stretched when you blow it up.

2. Inflate the balloon with one puff, just enough so it's not limp, but not so much that you notice the pressure building. That was easy, but from experience you know the next puff will be much harder.

3. Puff by puff, add more air. As soon as you feel it getting easier to inflate, stop and pinch the balloon closed. Each breath beyond this point will be easier. Add some more air to convince yourself that it is easier to blow up now. If you keep going, what will happen? Don't burst the balloon—we'll need it later.

Explanation

When you stretched the balloon with your hands, you had to apply force to get it to stretch. To get it to stretch twice as far, you had to pull with twice as much force. The balloon is exhibiting elastic behavior. The force required to stretch it is proportional to the distance stretched. This principle is known as Hooke's Law.

Stretching the balloon lengthens the long molecules in the latex rubber. The force you feel

continued on next page ➤

Blow Up a Balloon (continued)

is the molecules pulling to return to their relaxed position, like a stretched spring pulls to return to its relaxed position.

To inflate the balloon, you have to stretch the molecules again. The first puff filled out the balloon but didn't force the molecules to stretch. That was easy. The next puff stretched the molecules, and that was much harder.

Then it got easier. The next puff easily expanded the balloon, as did each succeeding puff. Although you were still stretching the rubber, the balloon exerted less pressure, which made it easier to inflate. As the balloon got bigger and had a larger diameter, less of its elastic force opposed the air pressure inside, so the pressure inside was lower.

If you had kept inflating it, you would have reached the limits of the rubber to expand. The last puff would have been difficult, as the rubber molecules

wouldn't have been able to stretch any more. That's when "pop!" occurs. Pushed beyond their ability to stretch, some of the molecules would break their bonds to adjoining molecules, letting the air escape in a sudden release or explosion.

Notice again that as you blow up a balloon, after the first breath, it becomes much harder to inflate. Once you've passed some point, it becomes easier to inflate. Most people have noticed this, but most haven't related it to other phenomena they have seen or can see. For instance, release an inflated balloon to watch its erratic flight. Just before it's empty, it exhibits a sudden extra blast of energy and then collapses. Here are two observations of the same phenomena: The pressure inside a balloon changes as you inflate it. When the balloon is quite small, it is hard to inflate because the elastic forces are pulling hardest, raising the internal pressure. Next is a demonstration of this effect.

Try This:
The Great Balloon Trick

This demonstration provokes interest because most people think that they know what will happen and are stunned when it doesn't. You will inflate two balloons, one very nearly full and the other just full enough so you've passed the hard part of blowing it up. Then you will connect the balloons as described below.

Once you have the balloons connected, ask an observer what will happen when you let air flow between them. Most people will guess that the small balloon will get bigger and the big balloon will get smaller so they end up about the same size. Nope!

Materials

- 2 latex balloons
- Glue
- 2 pop-open valves from water bottles or liquid detergent

Procedure

1. To make this demonstration much easier, start by collecting two pop-up lids from plastic bottles. Water and other drinks come in bottles with pop-up lids or valves on top. You open the bottle by pulling up on the valve to let the water out. The valves screw onto the bottles. Unscrew two of the lids and glue them together at their bases. You will need strong glue. Make sure you have laid a complete bead of glue around the base of one and then push the two together, base-to-base. It may take a few tries to get them to stick really well.

2. After the glue has cured, close the valves by pushing down on their tops. Inflate one balloon so it is nearly full and slide the mouth of the balloon over the ridge of one of the valves. When you release your grip on the neck of the balloon, it shouldn't lose air.

Now inflate the second balloon, but stop as soon as it gets easy to inflate. (Check out the experiment on page 17 if you're unsure of where to stop.)

continued on next page ➤

The Great Balloon Trick (continued)

3. Force the mouth of this balloon over the ridge of the other valve. If you don't hear air leaking you are ready to proceed. If you do hear a leak between the two valves, try to find and plug it with glue or tape.

4. Ask students which balloon will enlarge and which will shrink when you open the valves. Typical responses are that the balloons will "equalize." But what does that mean? Of course, they will have the same pressure once the valves are open, but what about the one parameter you can see: size? After they've guessed, open the two valves so air can flow freely between the two balloons.

Explanation

The bigger balloon gains air (gets bigger) at the expense of the smaller one. They don't equalize size, but they do equalize pressure. The smaller balloon had higher pressure; that's why it was harder to inflate at that size. The larger balloon was easier to inflate further, so it had lower pressure. In the demonstration, air moved from higher pressure to lower.

Wait for applause, and then take a bow.

Rocket-powered Applications:

Balloons at Work

Besides being great to play with, balloons are used in lots of work applications. For example, many types of life preservers have inflatable bags or balloons inside to provide buoyancy. SCUBA divers wear balloons called "buoyancy compensators" so they can stay neutrally buoyant in the water, which means they can stay at one depth without kicking. They also use balloons to raise heavy objects to the surface by attaching special lifting balloons to the objects and then filling the balloons with air from their SCUBA tanks. When you ship something that might break, you might use bubble wrap. It's a sheet of plastic with bubbles built in. Weather forecasters use balloons to lift their instruments into the atmosphere to take measurements. Your car won't get far without the tires being inflated. Look around you to see where else balloons are used.

Try This:

Make It Squeal

By the time they've reached the fourth grade, most kids have discovered how to annoy adults by making balloons squeal.

Materials

- Latex balloon

Procedure

Inflate a balloon and, holding the neck between your thumbs and forefingers, let the air out. It creates a noise that will send an agitated parent into orbit. This musical instrument uses the energy stored in the balloon to make music. How does it do that?

Explanation

The air escaping from the neck of the balloon pushes the two sides of the neck apart, stretching the latex. The stretched latex has an elastic restoring force that pulls the two sides back together, which shuts off the flow of air. The rapid opening and closing of the neck of the balloon generates sounds. Anyone watching should see, hear, and feel the vibrations to establish in their minds the relationships between vibrations and sound.

Try This:
Let It Go

Materials

• The latex balloon you used for the last activity

Procedure

Re-inflate the balloon and ask students what will happen when you release it. Everyone knows that it will fly willy-nilly around the room, generating much mirth and laughter. Release the balloon and then ask what happened.

Explanation

The observant student will report that the pressure inside the balloon forced air out the mouth. The elastic balloon pushed on the air inside, forcing it out. The escaping air exerted an equal and opposite force on the balloon, pushing it forward. This demonstrates Newton's Third Law of Motion: For every action, there is an equal and opposite reaction. Or, when two objects interact, the size of the force on each will be equal and the direction of the force on each will be in opposite directions. (See this book's Glossary for a description of Newton's three Laws of Motion.)

Why does the balloon sail wildly around the room? The neck of the balloon flops around as the balloon jerks forward sending the escaping air in different directions, which pushes the balloon in different directions. It takes some engineering to get the balloon to fly in a straight line, and that is the first model to try on page 40.

Try This:
Pop a Balloon I

Materials

• Latex balloon

Procedure

As soon as you inflate a balloon and tie the neck closed, someone will suggest popping it. Invite them to step forward to do that … by sitting on the balloon. (It helps if the balloon isn't fully inflated.) Or have them whack it with a mallet.

Explanation

They probably won't be able to pop it. Latex rubber balloons stretch and deform, making it difficult to pop them without using something sharp. But touch the sides with a pin, and "kaboom!"

The air inside an inflated balloon is at higher pressure than is the air outside. To inflate the balloon, you had to work to overcome the elastic forces of the balloon. The latex rubber stretches, but you have to force it to stretch by exhaling. If you let go of the opening, the air quickly escapes, flowing from the high pressure inside to the lower pressure outside. Popping a balloon creates a tiny hole that then rips wide as the air rushes to escape. Let's check what's happens when you pop a balloon.

Try This:
Pop a Balloon II

Materials
- Inflated latex balloon
- Long metal skewer

Procedure

1. First, let's not pop it. Take a long kitchen skewer made of either wood or metal (a 1/8-inch, or 3-millimeter, dowel also works well; sharpen one end). (If you're a student, seek adult help to handle the skewer.) Wave it around the partially inflated balloon to incite some energy in the class. Carefully force the sharp end into the balloon where the neck expands into the main body. You'll see that the latex isn't stretched rigidly there, and as the skewer enters, the latex forms a seal around it. Some air will leak out, but not much.

2. Now wave the balloon by holding onto the base of the skewer so everyone can see that it's inside the balloon. This is too cool, and they'll want to know how you did this.

3. If you're very careful and if the balloon is only half full, you can pass the skewer out through the very top of the balloon. Notice that this area isn't stretched rigid and can form a seal around the skewer.

4. Or, after passing the skewer into the balloon without popping it and causing some to think that it's a trick balloon, jab it out the side to pop it.

Whoa. That startled everyone who wasn't expecting the pop. Apologize and let's figure out what happened.

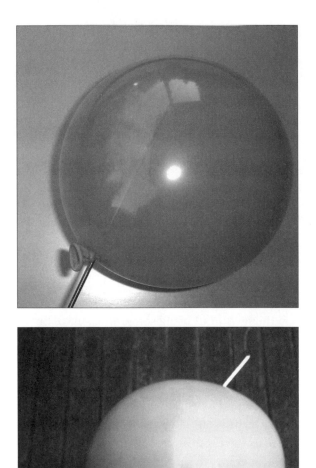

Explanation

Check out the side of the balloon. Do you find the tiny hole that the skewer made? No, you find a large rip. Once the air had a way to escape, it flowed out. As it did, it ripped the latex.

Look inside the balloon. It was dry before you inflated it. Now it's moist. Where did the water come from?

The moisture came from your breath. You inflated the balloon with air, including water vapor. When the balloon popped, the water vapor changed to water droplets. It *condensed* or changed states from a gas to a liquid. As air escaped, the pressure inside the balloon fell, and the drop in air pressure allowed the water vapor to condense.

Let's return to the first result of this experiment—everyone was startled. Most explosions occur when energy is released quickly and generates a wave that travels at the speed of sound. A dynamite explosion heats the surrounding air, expanding the volume and pressure of the air. That pressure moves away from the explosion at the speed of sound.

When the pressure wave arrives at your ears, it pushes on your eardrum and you hear the explosion. You may also feel the explosion as the wave hits your body.

You are probably familiar with the sound of one explosion: thunder. Thunder is caused by the rapid heating of the thin column of air surrounding a bolt of lightening. The hot air, as hot as 50,000°F (28,000°C), expands outward, hitting surrounding air molecules and setting them in motion. You hear and feel the thunder five seconds after lightning strikes a mile away.

Try popping (and not popping) a few balloons before doing the demonstration. It may take a few tries to get the balloon to pop when you want it to. Another way to stop a balloon from popping is to put a piece of clear tape on the side. Press it on firmly so it is almost invisible and then pass the skewer through the tape.

Try This:
Raise the Titanic, or a Book

From explosions we go to blowing things up—not as in destroying things, but as in raising them to a higher elevation. You can raise things up using air pressure or pressure in liquids. You could raise a copy of the movie *Titanic*, a book, or even the principal. In case you don't have a copy of *Titanic*, let's start by raising a book.

Materials

- Book
- Straw
- Plastic bag
- Strong adhesive tape
- Pencil

Procedure

1. Flatten the plastic bag so it contains no air. Fold over the open end about 1 inch (2.5 centimeters) down from the opening. Tape the fold in place. Use the pencil to poke a small hole along one side of the bag, just big enough for the straw to fit through. Insert the straw and tape it in place to make the bag airtight.

2. Plop the book on top of the bag. Now blow through the straw. You raised the book! And, it was pretty easy. Let the air escape from the bag and pile on a few more of your favorite books. See how many books you can raise.

Explanation

You used air pressure to lift the book. You spread the weight of the book (say it's a half-pound or quarter of a kilogram) over the surface area of the bag (my bag measured 10-1/2 by 12 inches [27 by 30 centimeters]). So the surface area of my bag is 10-1/2 times 12, or 126 square inches (813 square centimeters). To raise the book, all you have to do is increase the pressure inside the bag by more than the pressure exerted by the book: 0.5 pounds over 126 square inches, or 0.004 pounds per square inch (PSI). That's not much pressure.

If we added some other books, say 10 pounds total weight, the pressure we'd need would be 10 pounds over 126 square inches or 0.08 pounds per square inch. That's still too easy. Let's try raising something heavier.

Try This:
Elevate the Principal

Materials
- Large, heavy-duty trash bag, without trash
- Straws, one for each person helping
- Strong tape
- Large sheet of heavy cardboard
- 1 good-humored principal
- Pencil

Procedure

1. Spread the bag on the floor and push out any air. Even up the edges of the opening and fold them over about 1 inch (2.5 centimeters) down. Tape the fold in place.

2. With the pencil, make small holes along the edges of the bag so you can insert the straws. Make one hole for each person who will help you raise the principal. Insert the straws about an inch into the holes and tape them in place. You want to tape the straws securely so air won't leak around the edges of the holes.

3. Put a sheet of stiff cardboard on top of the bag and then ask your principal to lie down on the cardboard. Now, puff away. Have everyone blow into their straws. Tell them to pinch the straws while catching a breath so they keep the air in the bag. In just a few minutes you will have elevated the principal.

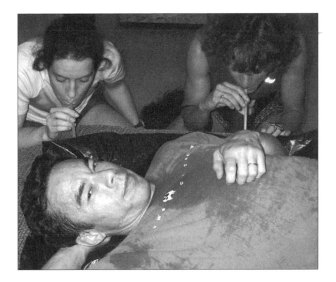

Explanation

Even though the principal may be a heavyweight in the field of education, when you spread his or her body weight over the area of the trash bag, the pressure (force or weight per area) is small. Using air pressure, you can lift things as heavy as your principal—and even heavier things.

Rocket-powered History:

Raise the Roof

Inflated dome roofs that are giant balloons cover some stadiums and tennis courts. Fans inside raise the air pressure to keep the roofs inflated. How can fans generate that much pressure? The pressure required is quite low as the force (weight of the roof) per surface area of the roof is low. Assume the roof weighs 2 pounds for every square foot section. The pressure required to support it would be 2 pounds divided by 144 square inches, or 0.014 PSI.

Try This:
The Plumber's Friend

We've demonstrated the power of air pressure by lifting weights easily. Now we can demonstrate the power of air pressure in holding things together.

Materials

- 2 toilet plungers, the simple and least expensive kind
- 2 lightweight students

Procedure

1. Push one plunger onto a smooth floor or wall. It sticks like it was glued in place. It sticks so strongly that a small elementary school student may not be able to remove it.

2. Bang two plungers together so they stick to one another and invite two small students to pull them apart. Big kids won't have a problem separating the plungers, but smaller kids often take a few tries before yanking them apart.

Explanation

If you ask students what held the plungers together, they will probably answer: "Suction!" A better answer is that atmospheric pressure held them together. The air in the atmosphere piled 50 miles high (80.47 kilometers) pushes down, compressing the air near the ground and raising air pressure from near zero (50 miles, or 80.47 kilometers, up) to about 14 pounds per square inch at sea level. By pushing the two plungers together, you expel air from the plungers and reduce the pressure inside. But outside, atmospheric air pressure pushes the

two plungers together with a force of 14 PSI times about 16 square inches (area of the plunger head), which is 224 pounds. If you were able to remove all the air from inside the two plungers, the difference in air pressure from outside (atmospheric) to inside (zero pressure) would be 224 pounds. That's much higher than the actual force required to separate the plungers because the pressure inside the plungers wasn't zero. You aren't able to force all the air from between the plungers. But the air that you did squeeze out reduced the pressure so that the ambient air pressure outside held the plungers together quite firmly.

Rocket-powered History:

The Vacuum

Imagine two teams of horses trying to pull apart a ball held together only by air pressure. That's how Otto von Guericke demonstrated his invention of an air pump in 1652. He used his pump to remove most of the air out of a sphere made of two halves. With the air removed, he created a vacuum (a space that contains no matter). Atmospheric pressure outside pressed the two parts together so strongly that even teams of horses weren't able to pull them apart. With the vacuum he was able to make, Guericke also demonstrated that candles needed air to burn, that mice needed air to breathe, and that sounds couldn't travel in a vacuum.

Rocket-powered Applications:

Want a Lift? Use Pressure

That's what mechanics do when they need to work on the underside of your car. Some elevators lift you from below by pumping you up. Some jacks, which are used to raise cars or lift houses to move them, use pressure too. Just like you were able to elevate the principal, you can raise really heavy things with pressure.

Lifts and elevators that use pressure to raise heavy things are called *hydraulic* lifts and elevators. *Hydraulic* means that they use liquids—usually oil called *hydraulic fluid*.

In many hydraulic machines the pressure is increased with an air compressor. To lift a car, the mechanic turns on an air compressor and it increases the pressure inside the pipes containing hydraulic fluid. As pressure increases, the hydraulic fluid pushes up a metal tube that lifts your car so the mechanic can look at the muffler.

Not all elevators use hydraulic lifts. Elevators in tall buildings are raised with cables pulling them from the roof. Shorter buildings with elevators tend to use hydraulic lifts. The machinery for hydraulic elevators is located in the elevator shaft below the car you ride in.

When you need to lift something really heavy, use pressure. And when you want to lift something light, you can use pressure there too.

Try This:

The Incredible Shrinking Balloon and Balloon Thermometer

This demonstration is an easy way to reinforce the concept that most materials expand when heated and shrink when cooled.

Materials

- Latex balloon
- 1-gallon milk jug
- Water and ice

Procedure

1. Pour some ice water in the jug. With the cap in place, shake the jug to cool all the air inside. Pour out the water and stretch the mouth of the balloon over the opening of the milk jug.

2. You could wait a few minutes for the air inside to warm up, or hold the jug under hot water in a sink or tub. As the air warms inside the tub, the balloon starts to inflate.

Explanation

Air pressure inside the jug and balloon builds as it warms. The added energy (heat) energizes the air molecules inside, making them move faster and have more collisions with the sides of the containers. Because the sides of the jug don't have much flexibility, the air will expand into the balloon, partially inflating it. This illustrates Charles's Law, which states that volume and temperature are inversely related. It says that the volume of a dry ideal gas is directly proportional to the absolute temperature (provided the amount of gas and the pressure remain fixed).

Try This:
Balloon in the Fridge

Here is another demonstration of the relationship between volume and temperature in a gas.

Materials

- 2 latex balloons, or

  2 plastic bags, a straw, and tape or rubber bands
- Freezer or refrigerator

Procedure

1. Inflate two identical balloons to the same size and tie them shut. If you don't have balloons handy, use two identical plastic bags. To inflate the bags, open them and scoop air by pulling them through the air. Draw the neck shut and hold it with one hand. Insert a straw and blow it up as fully as you can. Then quickly remove the straw and seal the neck with tape or a rubber band.

2. When you have filled two balloons or two bags, put one in a freezer or refrigerator. Keep the other at room temperature. (If you're trying this in an igloo, you should keep one at room temperature and hold the other above the oven door with the oven turned on!)

Explanation

In just a few minutes the balloon in the freezer or refrigerator collapses. Heat escaped from the air inside the balloon. The cold air now inside the balloon occupies less space than warm air did, so the balloon shrank.

Rocket-powered Applications:

How Do You Inflate Really Big Balloons?

Some of the biggest balloons are used to carry people through the air. Most common are hot-air balloons. This is the type you see floating through the air on weekend mornings. To lift the passengers and the basket, pilots fill the balloon with hot air. Because the hot air is less *dense* (has less weight per volume) than cooler air, the balloon weighs less than the surrounding air and it rises. When pilots want to stop gaining elevation, they let the air inside the balloon cool (turn off the heater) or vent some of the hot air through a slit in the balloon.

To get started, the pilot and crew lay out the nylon balloon on the ground. Before they can get the air inside the balloon hot, they have to fill the balloon with air. They use large fans, driven by gasoline engines, to fill it.

After there is enough air in the balloon to give it shape, pilots start heating the air inside the balloon. They turn on one or two burners, which use propane gas, and direct the flames and hot air into the mouth of the balloon. In a few minutes the balloon is standing up, like the balloon on top of the milk jug in one of the preceding experiments.

The pilot continues to heat the air inside the balloon until ready for lift-off. The ground crew helps hold the balloon down until passengers are aboard and ready for take-off.

Even small hot-air balloons hold a lot of air. Balloons that carry only two people need 60,000 cubic feet (1,700 cubic meters) of air. These balloons typically have diameters of about 50 feet (15 meters).

Try This:
Make a Hot-air Balloon

Materials

- Plastic bag, the kind you put vegetables in at the store, or a plastic bag from a dry cleaner
- Clear plastic tape
- 1/8-inch, or 3-millimeter, balsa wood strips
- 4 paper clips
- Teakettle
- Water
- Stove or hot plate

⚠ IMPORTANT SAFETY NOTE

This activity requires constant adult supervision because of the possibility of being burned by steam or by a hot teapot.

Procedure

1. Put some water in the teapot and heat the pot on the stove. While the water is heating, attach four paper clips evenly spaced around the opening of the plastic bag.

2. If using a bag from a dry cleaner, find all the holes in the bag and seal them by folding a flap of adjacent plastic over the hole and taping it in place. To keep the mouth of the dry cleaner's bag open, make an X with two thin (1/8-inch, or 3-millimeter) strips of balsa wood and tape the two pieces together. Tape the four ends into the mouth of the bag.

3. When steam is coming out of the spout of the teapot, have an adult assistant hold the bag by the handles so it catches the steam. Steam is very hot and you need to keep your hands away from it.

4. As the bag fills with hot air and water vapor, let go of the balloon. The bag will float up toward the ceiling. The colder the room is, the higher the bag will float.

continued on next page ➤

Make a Hot-air Balloon (continued)

Explanation

The hot and moist air coming from the tea kettle's spout is less dense than the cooler and drier surrounding air. When this less dense air fills the bag, it will tug upward to rise.

The four paper clips (or the balsa wood sticks) provide enough weight to keep the bag's opening pointing down so the lighter air inside doesn't spill out. You can make much larger hot-air balloons that will rise 100 feet (30 meters) or more by making a balloon out of tissue paper.

Rocket-powered History:

The First Launch

The first people to fly were not the Wright Brothers, but a pair of French brothers about 100 years before the airplane inventors were born. Jacques Etienne and Joseph Michel Montgolfier made the first hot-air balloon. They conducted two experiments without people on board, and then in 1783 they sent up a balloon with two people. The balloon ride lasted nearly a half-hour above Paris. Once they showed that people could fly, many others started experimenting with hot-air balloons.

A Note On:

Helium-filled Balloons

The other type of big balloon is filled with a light gas, instead of hot air. The gas-filled balloons you buy are filled with helium, a gas that is less dense than air. Because it is less dense than air, the balloon and gas weigh less than the same volume of air and it rises. We say it is buoyant.

In addition to being less dense than air, helium molecules are quite small. They're so small that they leak through the sides of a latex balloon. After a day or two so much helium has leaked out that the balloon is flat—unless you got a helium grade latex or foil balloon. The microscopic openings in these balloons are much smaller than in an ordinary latex balloon.

It is common, but incorrect, to call foil balloons Mylar. Foil balloons are made of nylon that has been coated on one side with a plastic (polyethylene, also used to make light plastic bags) and a layer of metal on the other. The polyethylene greatly slows the flow of helium through the sides of the balloon and the metal surface reflects radiated heat so the balloon doesn't expand and explode.

Rocket-powered History:

The Biggest Blow-up I

The biggest helium-filled balloons are used inside airships. Blimps and dirigibles can float through the air because their gasbags or balloons contain helium, making them lighter than the surrounding air. The biggest airships were about 1,000 feet (300 meters) long. Be glad you don't have to inflate one of those.

Rocket-powered History:

The Biggest Blow-up II

Some studies have shown that helium balloons rise to between 28,000 and 30,000 feet (8,500 to 9,100 meters) before bursting. This is the altitude at which commercial airlines fly. The balloons rise at about 1,050 feet per minute (320 meters per minute), so they can be blown quite high before bursting.

In 1994 a film company released 1,592,744 helium-filled balloons at the same time. We don't suggest you try to top this record. Today releasing balloons is discouraged because sea turtles and other animals can choke on the long-lasting plastic and rubber.

Rocket-powered Applications:

Weather Balloons

Meteorological scientists launch their instruments into the sky using helium-filled balloons. Some long-distance recreational balloonists also use helium rather than hot-air balloons.

Try This:
Can You Give Me a Lift?

Here is a simple demonstration or activity for younger students.

Materials
- 2 or more helium-filled balloons
- Large plastic bag
- Paper or Styrofoam cup
- String
- Paper clips

Procedure

1. Use a plastic bag that is big enough to hold several helium-filled balloons. Tie two or three pieces of string onto the plastic around the opening of bag and tie them (or tape them) to the cup. The cup becomes the gondola of the balloon. Add one helium balloon to the bag and see if it has enough lift to raise the cup off the ground. If not, add a second helium-filled balloon.

2. Once you have the cup in the air, see if you can balance the balloon by adding paper clips or pennies to the cup. When you get it balanced, watch as the balloon moves around the room, pushed and pulled by the air currents. Above a heating duct or radiator, the balloon might get caught in an updraft. What happens when someone opens or shuts a door to the room? Can you predict how your balloon will respond? Can you make a map of air currents in the room? This is the same mapping concept that ocean scientists use to track currents: they follow "drifters" in the water.

Explanation

Getting the balloons and gondola to stay at the same level shows that they are neutrally buoyant. That is, the upward buoyant forces (from the lighter-than-air gas, helium) are balanced by the downward force of gravity. This same combination of balloons and weights would not be neutrally buoyant if the air were much warmer or colder. In colder air, because it is denser, the same balloon system would rise.

Model to Make:
Launch a Balloon Rocket

Zoom into the next room or across your yard with a balloon rocket. Like all rockets, balloon rockets move forward by pushing gas (in this case, air) backward.

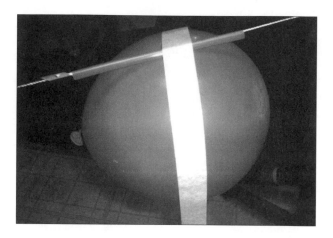

Materials

- Latex balloons
- Sturdy string
- Straws
- Masking tape

Procedure

1. Set up the flight line. Stretch the string between two trees or fenceposts outside or between doorknobs or cabinet handles inside. Tie one end of the string to an anchor (tree or doorknob), thread a straw onto the string, and then tie the second end of the string to the far anchor. Make the string as taut as you can without damaging the anchors or breaking the string. To do this, tie a loop into the string 3 feet (1 meter) from the second anchor. Loop the string around the anchor and back through the loop. Pull on the free end of the string to tension the string, and then secure it with an overhand knot. Make sure that you've chosen a location where people won't hurt themselves by walking into the string.

2. Take two strips of masking tape about 1 inch (2.5 centimeters) long and tape them to your shirt or pants. This isn't to make a new fashion statement; it's to reduce the stickiness of the tape so you can remove it without ripping the balloon later. Inflate a balloon and hold the neck shut. Peel the tape off your clothes and use the two strips to attach the balloon to the straw. The balloon nozzle should be pointing away from the intended direction of travel.

3. Release the nozzle. Lift off!

Explanation

The balloon should have traveled at least 20 to 30 feet (6 to 9 meters). The air at higher pressure inside the balloon pushed out the mouth, launching the balloon forward. If the balloon didn't fly well, try it again and make sure the balloon is aligned parallel to the string. If the balloon isn't aligned, the balloon will spin around the guide string and not go anywhere.

See how far you can get a balloon rocket to travel. Have student teams measure and record the distance of each launch. Will a two-balloon rocket go twice as far as one? Better check it out.

Learning Moments

Some students may attach the balloon facing the wrong direction. Let them release the balloon and realize their error. Then help them understand by asking in what direction the force has to be to propel the rocket along the string. Balloons attached somewhat sideways to the straw will twirl around the string as they move forward. Ask teams what causes the spinning and help them recognize that it represents a loss of energy that could propel the rocket further.

Rocket-powered History:

First American in Space

Commander Alan Shepard was the first American to fly in space. He launched aboard a Redstone rocket on May 5, 1961.

Model to Make:
Two-stage Balloon Rockets

If you tried to use two round balloons for a balloon rocket on a string, you discovered how difficult it is to get them to travel as far as a single-balloon rocket. Here is a way to use two balloons.

Materials

- Long, thin party balloons
- String
- Tape
- Large Styrofoam coffee cups
- Balloon inflater (pump)—these balloons are tough to inflate

Procedure

1. Set up the guide string as before, but consider making it longer and thread two straws onto the string before tying it.

2. Inflate one party balloon and tape it to the lead straw.

3. Have someone hold the neck shut while you prepare the second balloon. While inflating the second one, place a cylinder of Styrofoam (cut from a coffee cup) around the closed end of the balloon.

4. Continue inflating the balloon and tape it to the second straw.

5. Force the neck of the first balloon between the Styrofoam cylinder and the second balloon, so the pressure of the second balloon holds the neck of the first balloon shut.

6. Release the first balloon to test the fit.

7. When ready to launch, release your grip on the neck of the second balloon. It serves as the first stage of this rocket, stopping after it has accelerated and releasing the second stage that travels much farther.

Model to Make:

Rocket Dust

Here is a fun activity that shows that the contents of the balloon are forced out of the mouth as the balloon moves forward.

Materials

- Balloon rockets (from either of the previous models)
- Flour

Procedure

1. Starting with a fresh balloon, add a scoop of flour to the balloon. To get the flour in, pour it into a paper funnel or cone whose narrow end has been inserted into the mouth of the balloon.

2. Inflate the balloon and tape it to the straw on the string. Just before releasing it, shake up the balloon to get the flour floating in the air inside.

3. Release and watch the trail of flour smoke.

Model to Make:
Balloon Rocket Cars

This challenging activity can engage anyone as young as those in elementary school and as advanced as graduate students. Getting the car to move is somewhat challenging, but getting it to go really far takes persistence and good engineering.

Materials

- Cardboard
- Wheels
- Dowels
- Straws
- Hot-glue guns
- Balloons
- Tape
- Vinyl tube (1/4 and 3/8 inch, or 6 to 9 millimeters, in diameter)
- Rubber bands
- Measuring tape
- Scissors

Plastic wheels without end caps allow a dowel to pass through completely (also allowing three-wheel cars). Kelvin.com carries wheels that fit onto 1/8-inch (3-millimeter) dowels (which are lso available from Kelvin.com). These fit through standard drinking straws that can be glued or taped to the bottom of a piece of cardboard.

Procedure

1. Lay out a racecourse on a smooth floor. Put down a piece of masking tape down as the start line and mark distances every 10 feet (3 meters) along the course in one direction.

2. Introduce the challenge (design, build, test, and improve model cars to go as far as possible using the energy stored in one inflated balloon) and show the class both the racecourse and the materials available. Have students form two-person teams.

3. Before they add an engine, have each team demonstrate that their car moves in a straight line and that it has no major design flaws that will retard its progress. Then issue one balloon. (Later, after a team successfully demonstrates its car, consider letting team members have a second balloon if they request it. Contrary to their expectations, two-balloon cars rarely travel as far as do one-balloon cars).

4. Have teams test and improve their rocket cars as often as they can in the time available. They should measure and record each test (how far the car went and what change they made), either on data sheets you provide or on the board. Then, before making another test, they should make one and only one improvement to their model. Although the stated challenge is to get cars to travel as far as possible, the real objective is to get students doing science (enthusiastically) and following a method.

5. Teams that work quickly and develop cars that go far often come up with creative extensions. Encourage them and try to provide additional materials to facilitate their inquiry.

Learning Moments ·ᵠ·

Most students will opt for four-wheel cars, so encourage them to think of other designs (three-wheel) for the added challenge. Vinyl tubing is available in short lengths at hardware stores and on plumbing supply sites on the World Wide Web.

Also, this activity works best in pairs, so have students form two-person teams. Having them select teammates works well for about 90 percent of the students; the others need direction to form teams that will work.

continued on next page ➤

Balloon Rocket Cars (continued)

Learning Moments

There are several opportunities to transform the physical learning experience into words and diagrams and thus create understanding on multiple levels. First is getting the car to travel. Some students will glue axles to the car bodies (cardboard) or will have wheels rubbing against the cardboard or straws, resulting in short runs. Reduction of friction is fundamental to getting good distance.

Another learning opportunity is getting the car to travel in a straight line. The source of most problems is misaligned axles. Ask students how their family car turns into a fast-food restaurant—the driver turns the front axle in the direction of French fries. Look at the underside of the car—usually the misalignment is obvious. You are teaching them to relate results with causes (fundamental to scientific inquiry) and to think how similar machines work.

Some teams will point their car so the balloon will blow it backward. Without your intervention, they will giggle and turn the car around after making the mistake. Help them think through this experience by asking what direction the balloon's exhaust will blow. Then ask: If the balloon is pushing in one direction, what direction will the car go? Or, if you're roller-skating and want to move to the north, what direction do you push with your feet? South. (Remember Newton's Third Law of Motion.)

Teams may opt to use the vinyl tube or a straw to direct the exhaust of the balloon. They may not, however, orient the tube or straw exactly opposite to the direction of intended travel: The tube may point up or down or to one side. Question them to help them understand that the direction of the force is as important as the magnitude of the force. Pushing directly to the side won't provide forward motion; pushing partially to one side will apply only a fraction of the available force to move the car forward.

After teams have made and tested models, ask them if they think that rockets could power automobiles. What problems would such cars have? They would have the same issues that students encountered in making their models work: keeping the car moving in the desired direction. Interested students can check Internet sites for the various urban legends about backyard mechanics strapping rocket engines to their cars.

One key element of this activity is to post the longest runs. Prizes aren't needed. Merely posting the record will encourage teams to try harder to beat it. In their quest to set the record, they will encounter new engineering problems to solve and will learn more. Let the rewards of record-setting work in a positive way to encourage learning.

Model to Make:

More Fun with Rocket Cars

Teams can use (or not use) short (1- to 2-inch, or 2.5- to 5-centimeter) lengths of vinyl tube. It makes it easier to control the direction of balloon exhaust. And, it provides an additional series of experiments to run.

Providing a selection of tubing with different diameters allows teams to test for the optimum diameter. They could measure the distance traveled (repeating and averaging at least three runs with each size) for all the sizes available and graph the results.

Using tubing of one diameter, teams could test for the optimal length. They could start with a long piece (say, 8 inches, or 20 centimeters) and measure the distance the car travels (at least three tests at each length and averaging the total) and then cut it by 1 inch (2.5 centimeters) and re-testing. A graph would summarize their data and they would describe their findings in writing.

"Rocket Cars" is a fun activity that gets kids doing science. They run experiments of their own inquiry, make changes, and re-test, collecting data that they report graphically and in writing. Hurray! Here is science in the classroom.

Model to Make:
Rocket Boats

The rocket car and boat are conceptually similar activities. The car provides more opportunities for data collecting and analysis. However, rocket boats can reinforce the learning (Newton's Third Law of Motion) and demonstrate that travel through water is somewhat different than on land.

Materials

- Empty paper cartons (from milk or juice)
- Sharp knife
- Bendable straws
- Hot-glue gun
- Tape
- Nail or awl
- Wading pool or swimming pool

IMPORTANT SAFETY NOTE ⚠️

This activity requires the use of a knife. For students in grades 6 and lower, adults should do the cutting in advance of the activity. Older students can use scissors to do their own cutting, with adult supervision, of course.

Procedure

1. Teams of students design, build, and test model boats powered by a single inflated balloon. To make boat hulls, use a sharp knife to cut milk cartoons in half lengthwise. Each cartoon makes two hulls.

2. The goal is to get each boat to propel itself across the largest (safe) watery expanse you have available. An ideal would be one without waves, wind, or current that would allow measurements of distance. Absent the ideal, a large wading pool or water-filled rain gutter (on the ground) can suffice. (Hardware stores sell plastic rain gutters and end caps that make good and safe test tanks.)

3. The most difficult part of this activity is sealing the balloon to the bendable straw. Fold the neck of the balloon onto itself (with the straw inside) and then tape it in place.

4. Some teams will vent the balloon/straw motor into the water (through a hole in the deck or transom of the boat) and others will vent it into the air. Restricting the air flow with a paper clip or staple across the end of the straw often increases the distance traveled and provides the auditory enjoyment of a "putt-putt" motor sound.

5. Have teams measure how far their boat travels and record this measurement along with the changes they make to improve the distance.

Learning Moments 💡

An unexpected opportunity occurs when students consider making a hole in the deck for a straw to penetrate. Typical expectations are that the boat will then sink. Encourage them to try this (they can cover the hole with tape or with hot glue fill in the hole later) to disabuse them of this idea.

Rocket boats, like rocket cars, is a demonstration of Newton's Third Law of Motion. To work well, the balloon must be venting directly opposite to the intended direction of travel. Here, however, there are no wheels to provide friction to keep the vehicle from turning. A straw pointing sideways will drive the bow of the boat in the same direction. That is, the boat will turn around its center of drag, the fore-aft center of the hull. Pushing the air toward the left (port for your mariners) will push the stern to the right (Newton was right), but push the bow to the left. That is, the boat will pivot around its center. Explaining this in words is much less rewarding than experiencing it with models (and then adding the words).

Point out to teams that their boats experience a sudden increase in speed just before the balloon empties. Refer to "The Great Balloon Trick" on page 19 for an explanation of this effect.

Some teams might want to add a sail to their boat and have the balloon blow onto the sail to provide propulsion. Position yourself by the test tank when they are ready to test their boat, and ask questions to provoke their thinking and understanding of why this won't work.

Chapter 3

Powered by Jets of Air

Jets are streams of fluid pushed out from a constricted area. You would be correct in pointing out that balloons issue jets of air. You discovered jets of air in Chapter 2's

activities. In this chapter we will use jets of air to play music (you may call it noise) and to launch rockets. But first, a demonstration!

Try This:
Launch Ping-pong Balls

Jets of air can launch Ping-pong balls 50 feet (15 meters) or more. Here is a series of demonstrations on the principles of flight as well as air pressure and ballistics.

Materials

- Shop vac or blower, with a nozzle that fits the PVC pipe
- 1-inch-diameter (2.54-centimeter) PVC pipe
- 1-inch-diameter (2.54-centimeter) PVC "T" joint
- Hacksaw
- Ping-pong balls

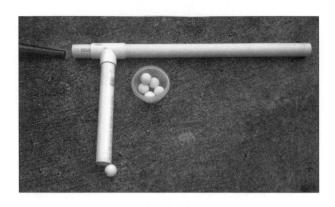

IMPORTANT SAFETY NOTE ⚠️

This activity requires the use of a sharp cutting tool. For students in grades 6 and lower, adults should do the cutting in advance of the activity. Older students can use scissors to do their own cutting, with adult supervision, of course.

Procedure

1. To make the launcher, you will need to cut three pieces of PVC pipe to fit into the three sides of the "T" joint. First, cut one of the arms. This can be about 3 feet (1 meter) long. Exact length is not critical for this piece and it would be fun to experiment with different lengths, testing how far the launcher projects balls.

2. Cut the center leg (pick up tube) for the "T" to be about 18 inches (.45 meter). This length isn't critical either, but the next length is.

3. The third piece needs to be just long enough so the shop vac nozzle will almost reach the edge of the opening from the pick-up tube. Insert the nozzle into the "T" and hold it so the end of the nozzle almost reaches the center hole. Estimate the length of pipe you will need to hold the nozzle in this position. Cut the pipe, insert it into the "T," and see if it positions the nozzle correctly.

4. Push the pieces of PVC pipe into the "T" valve. There is no need to glue the pieces together; the pressure fit will hold them.

5. To launch, insert the nozzle into the third piece of pipe. Use one hand to hold the nozzle and pipe together and use the other hand to support the long (launch) pipe. Have someone turn on the blower. Being careful to aim the long end of the launcher away from people and breakable stuff, release a Ping-pong ball up the pick-up leg.

Explanation

The shop vac blows a stream of fast-moving air through the pipe and out the far end. The fast-moving air has lower pressure than outside the pipe. If you put your hand over the pick-up leg, you'll feel the suction. The low pressure pulls balls up the pick-up leg, against the force of gravity.

This is the Bernoulli effect. Fast-moving air is associated with reduced pressure and this sucks balls up the pipe. The low pressure in the "T" caused by the shop vac pulls air (and Ping pong balls) up the tube.

People often invoke the Bernoulli effect to describe how airplane wings generate lift. The argument goes that the shape of the wing causes air to pass over the top of the wing at faster speeds than underneath. This fast-moving air causes or is caused by a reduced pressure that sucks the wing upward. There are better ways to describe how wings generate lift (see Donald Anderson and Scott Eberhardt's *Understanding Flight* in the References at the back of this book), but the Ping-pong launcher does demonstrate the Bernoulli effect.

Once a ball has risen up the pick-up leg, it is blown out the long arm tube. A long tube allows a ball time to fully accelerate and to fly far. A very long tube would reduce the airspeed through friction, with the sidewalls making the ball travel a shorter distance. Finding the optimal launch tube length would be a fun science fair project.

Try This:

Twirling Sounds

Have you seen the plastic tubes you whirl around in a circle to make neat sounds? The tubes have ridges that generate the sound. You can get sounds the same way using plastic drinking straws that have ridges.

Just hold the tube by one end and spin it around. Spinning the tube throws air out the distant end. In a similar tube without ridges, you wouldn't hear the sounds. The air hitting the ridges causes air molecules to vibrate and you hear that as the steady tone. To change tones, spin the tube faster or slower.

Model to Make:

Two-reed Flute

This simple instrument conveys instantly the relationship between sound and vibrations. And, it helps students understand how sounds are generated.

Materials

- Straws
- Scissors
- Tape

Procedure

Basic Model

1. Chew on one end of the straw to flatten it enough so you can cut it. With the scissors, cut from the side of the straw to the center of the end. Start the cut about 1/4 inch (.6 centimeter) from the end of the straw. Then repeat the cut on the other side so you end up with two sharp points at the end of the straw.

2. Pop this end back in your mouth and blow through the straw. If you don't get a wonderful sound at first, change the position of the straw in your mouth. You can also chomp on the end once or twice more to make sure it is pliable and able to vibrate. Playing a straw flute is one of life's simple pleasures and is well worth your time to master.

3. Alas, the range of notes is limited to one. No matter how hard you blow, you make only one note of music. It's the length of the straw that determines what that note is, so let's change the length of the straw.

The Shortee

Once you have developed the skill to play the regular straw flute, you will love to do this. But be aware that there is danger here. You could cut off your nose and that would ruin all the fun you're having, so be careful.

Take a deep breath and play a note with your straw flute. Hold that thought and note. With the scissors and with care (not to cut off your nose), chop an inch off the end of the straw. The pitch of the sound goes up.

Cut off another inch and the pitch rises again. Keep cutting until you have just a nib of a straw left and your lips tickle when you play it. This will get everyone's attention. It will also strongly relate sound to vibrations as you remember the tickling of your lips while you played the flute. And it will demonstrate the relationship between the tone (frequency) of a sound and the length of the tube that is making it.

continued on next page ➤

Two-reed Flute (continued)

The Longee

Now that you know what happens if you make the flute shorter, you can figure out what's going to happen if you make it longer.

Make a basic straw flute and get it working. Cut a 1/4-inch (1-centimeter) slit in the end of a second straw so you can slide it onto the end of your flute. Tape it in place with a piece of masking tape. Whoa, the sound that it produces is awesome.

If a two-straw flute is fun, a three-straw flute must be more fun. Give it a try. Why quit with three? The world record (we assume it's the world record) is held by the author—15 straws. See if you can break that.

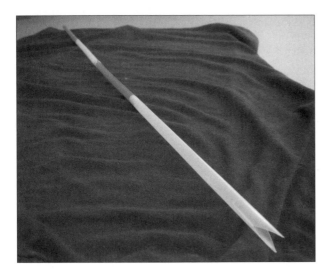

Slide Flute

Make a slide flute by slitting a straw along its length and sliding it onto the basic model straw flute. Pull it in and out to make different tunes.

Add some holes. Use an awl to make holes in a straw flute and cover and uncover them to change the tone.

Explanation

You made a lot of neat sounds that had everyone giggling. In each case blowing through the straw got the two reeds vibrating. The length of the straw determined whether you heard high notes or low. The longest flutes played the lowest (slowest vibrating) pitched notes.

This instrument behaves like a clarinet. As you blow on the reeds, you get them to flutter back and forth. As they move they periodically constrict the flow of air, changing both the flow and air pressure inside the straw. This vibration generates the sound.

The length of the straw determines the pitch of frequency of the sound. The wavelength of the sound produced is about four times the length of a straw. For a standard drinking straw 11 inches (28 centimeters) long, the sound wave will have a wavelength of 44 inches (112 centimeters). The frequency of a sound wave with a wavelength of 44 inches (112 centimeters) is about 310 Hz (using a speed of sound for 72°F, or 22°C, at sea level). Cutting an inch off the straw raises the frequency to about 340 Hz. Adding a second straw makes the length about 21 inches (53 centimeters). This lowers the frequency to about 160 Hz.

Making an assumption about the speed of sound (several Web sites calculate it based on temperature, humidity, and elevation) and knowing the wavelength (based on the length of the straw) lets us calculate the frequency of the sound produced. The frequency (in Hz or cycles per second) multiplied by the wavelength equals the speed of sound.

When you cut the straw flute shorter, you were able to play higher notes. In musical instruments you blow to play, you also lengthen or shorten the path air takes to make different notes. In flutes, you cover and uncover the finger holes making the air travel different lengths to escape. The saxophone and clarinet have keys you depress to open holes so air can come out changing the length. Trombones change the length of the tube by sliding in and out, and trumpets achieve the same result by opening or closing sections of tube with finger valves. Each has a different way of changing the path air takes, but all operate with the same physics as your straw flute.

Learning Moments

As students make their own flutes, ask if they can feel the sounds in their lips. They should feel the vibrations. Ask them what causes sounds and they should instinctively answer that vibrations cause sounds. As they get ready to modify their straws, have them predict what will happen to the sound. You might have them write down the experiment (for example, cutting the straw shorter) and their prediction. Forcing them to think about the experience in other cognitive styles will help them understand and remember.

Model to Make:
A Whistle

If you have a police whistle, dig it out and take a look at it. See any reeds? There aren't any. Notice any moving parts?

Whistles make noise when you blow hard enough through them to cause air to swirl. When you blow a whistle ("Please, not in the house."), the air swirls around after hitting the edge downstream from the mouthpiece. It is the air itself that moves and causes sound. The size of the whistle determines the size of the swirls and the tone of the whistle.

The whistle would work without the ball inside. The ball spins around and, sometimes, blocks the opening. This changes the sound of the whistle, making it warble.

Materials

- Piece of paper, or

  Blade of grass

Procedure

1. Cut a piece of office or notebook paper about 2 inches (5 centimeters) long and 1/4 inch (1 centimeter) wide.

2. Hold the piece taut horizontally with the thumb and forefinger of each hand.

3. Starting with your hands positioned below your lips, blow hard while raising your hands. Find the place where you get a whistle. You have to hold the paper so it doesn't move.

4. Try substituting a blade of grass for a piece of paper.

Explanation

Blowing across the sharp edge of the paper or grass causes air molecules to roll or swirl and produce sounds. This type of sound maker is called an *aerodynamic whistle*, like the police whistle. More common are non-aerodynamic devices such as flutes, guitars, or drums. These instruments have vibrating parts, reeds, strings, or drumheads, and those parts vibrate the air around them. Aerodynamic devices don't have vibrating parts. Instead they get the air itself to vibrate and that causes sounds. Another aerodynamic whistle is a whistling teapot. 'Tis time for tea and a good whistle.

Model to Make:

A Foghorn

You'll be blown away by the sounds that come out of a film canister. Your students will drive you nuts with these—so only make them at the end of the day. The good news is that students can see, feel, and hear the vibrations and can relate them to the sounds they produce.

Materials

- Film canisters
- Drill bits
- Straws
- Hot-glue gun
- Latex balloons or gloves
- Rubber bands
- Single-hole punch
- Drill bit

Procedure

1. Make a hole in the side of a film canister with the single-hole punch. Next, make a hole in the bottom of the canister with a drill bit. Size the bit so the hole will just barely admit a straw. You can drill the hole by holding the bit in one hand and turning the canister around with the other hand.

⚠ IMPORTANT SAFETY NOTE

For students in grades 3 or below, pre-drill the hole using a drill and bit.

2. Cut a latex balloon or glove to give a large flat section of a single ply. Lay this over the open end of the canister, smooth out the wrinkles, and hold in place with a rubber band wrapped around the canister.

3. Push a straw up through the hole in the bottom of the canister. Position it so it touches and slightly raises the balloon that is stretched across the canister. Blow with gusto through the hole in the side of the canister. "Wow, that's loud!"

4. Adjust the sounds by adjusting the pressure on the balloon head—pushing up or lowering the straw. You can hot-glue this straw in place, although doing so makes it difficult to change the pressure on the diaphragm. Cut or lengthen this straw to change the pitch.

5. To make blowing easier, insert a short section of straw into the side hole and hot-glue it in place.

continued on next page ➤

A Foghorn (continued)

Bigger and more impressive foghorns use the same design, but substitute a piece of 1/2-inch-diameter (1.2-centimeter) PVC pipe for the straw that protrudes through the bottom. Try an 8-foot-long (2.4-meter) piece of pipe to get truly impressive, low tones.

Explanation

Watch the rubber diaphragm (balloon or glove) rise and fall as you blow. You can see the vibrations that are causing the sounds you hear.

As you blow, the air inside has no place to go because the balloon is resting on the top of the straw, blocking any air from leaving. As the pressure inside increases, it raises the balloon off the straw. This lets some air escape through the straw, but it also reduces the pressure inside. With reduced pressure, the balloon's elastic contracts, shutting this air pressure valve. The balloon lifts up and falls down many times a second, so you can see it only as a blur.

Learning Moments

As students get creative with their foghorns, have them think about how the sounds are being made and how their modifications will change the sounds. Get them to express in words and diagrams the science they are experiencing. Encourage them to try some creative ways to make different notes. They could lengthen the path escaping air takes by taping straws onto the end of the first straw. They could cut holes in the straw to cover and uncover with their fingers.

Even more creative is to replicate this model at different scales and with different materials. Using PVC pipe instead of straws is the first thing to try. Try using an instant oats (cylindrical) container in place of the film canister. Then large diameter tubes, like a vacuum cleaner or swimming pool hose, could replace the straw or PVC pipe.

Model to Make:
Straw Rockets

This is a fun activity that kids enjoy. They make and launch rockets made of "fat" straws by blowing through regular straws.

Materials

- "Fat" straws
- Regular drinking straws
- Masking tape
- Paper clips
- Index cards
- Safety glasses

You can find "fat" straws at restaurant supply stores. They have larger diameters than regular straws and come in boxes of a few hundred. If these are hard to find, have kids make their own rockets by rolling a quarter sheet of office paper around a pencil and taping it into a cylinder.

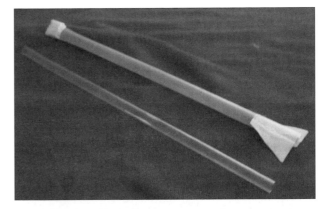

⚠
IMPORTANT SAFETY NOTE
Be sure that all participants wear safety goggles during this activity.

Procedure

1. To make the rockets, fold over one end of a "fat" straw and tape the end to the rest of the straw, thus sealing off that end. Add fins, either made of masking tape (folded over onto itself) or index cards, to the other end and launch. Experiment with adding weights and with the size and position of the fins to see which design gives the longest launches.

2. Establish a launch line with a piece of masking tape on the floor. To make measuring easier, mark the distance from the launch line every 5 feet (or 2 meters) with a piece of tape. Provide kids with a meter or yardstick to measure between adjacent marks, and have them record their distances on the board.

continued on next page ➤

Straw Rockets (continued)

3. They can launch as often as they would like, provided they follow the rules. After each launch, they must measure the distance and record it, think how to improve it, and make one change to the rocket. The goal is get their rocket to go as far as possible and for them to understand what impact each change made.

4. Have kids show their best rocket and explain what they learned. Challenge them to continue working at home on their rockets and have them bring in what they make to test/demonstrate.

To make a launcher instead of using lungpower to launch straw rockets, drill a hole through the cap of a 1-liter water bottle and insert the end of a bendable straw into the hole. Hot-glue the straw in place. Slide the rocket onto the other end of the straw and squeeze the bottle to launch. Blow through the straw to re-inflate the bottle.

Model to Make:
Pneumatic-blast Rockets

Kids and adults find this activity extremely fun. Your students will want to keep working on their pneumatic-blast rockets, and many will continue working at home.

You can use pneumatic-blast rockets in several different ways:

- As a great vehicle for learning science content covering motion, position, forces, energy, and energy transformations, plus experiencing the methods of science

- As a way to introduce science fair projects. This activity takes kids from experiment design through graphing and reporting.

- As a fun reward or for special "science day" activity

IMPORTANT SAFETY NOTE
This activity requires adult supervision and the use of safety goggles.

Materials

You can make and launch hundreds of rockets for an investment of about $1. The critical materials are free: empty, 2-liter soda bottles, used bicycle inner tubes, and scrap paper. You do need to purchase some PVC pipe, but the cost is pennies per foot. You don't need to make a stand-up launcher, but if you do, the additional cost is only a few dollars. Here's the total list of materials:

- 2-liter soda bottles
- Bike inner tube
- 3/4-inch-diameter, or 2-centimeter, PVC pipe, schedule 200
- 8.5-x-11-inch (22-x-28-centimeter) paper
- Index cards or business cards (for fins)
- Masking tape
- Paper clips
- Duct tape
- Scissors
- Hacksaw

For the launcher:

- A pine board (4 feet long, 10 inches wide by 1 inch deep, or 1.2 meters long, 25 centimeters wide by 2.5 centimeters deep)
- 2.5-inch-diameter (5-centimeter) PVC pipe, 4 feet (1.2 meters) long
- 2-x-4-inch (5-x-10-centimeter) stud for support feet
- 2-inch-long (5-centimeter) bolt, two nuts and washers
- Hot-glue gun
- Drill and bits
- Protractor
- Safety glasses

continued on next page ➤

Pneumatic-blast Rockets (continued)

Procedure

1. To make the rocket fuselage, roll a piece of scrap office paper around the outside of a 10-inch-long (25-centimeter-long) piece of the PVC pipe. Loosen the paper so the pipe slides easily through it. To keep the paper from unrolling, tape the edge of the paper with three short pieces of masking tape.

2. You need to close one end of the rocket to make it airtight. Hold one end of the fuselage (the paper cylinder) between your thumbs and middle fingers, and pinch inward with your index fingers. Just before your index fingers touch, pinch your thumbs together with your middle fingers to shut the tube. Tape this with a short piece of masking tape. It's not yet airtight, so fold the end over and tape it down against the fuselage.

3. The fuselage is now airtight. You can test it blowing into the end of the tube. No air escapes, so the fuselage is ready.

4. You can launch these rockets with a minimalist launcher made of a 2-liter soda bottle, bike inner tube, and 10-inch-long (25-centimeter-long) piece of PVC pipe. Get the inner tube from a bike store; often they can give you a few that they are throwing out. Find one that doesn't have a hole in it and cut away the valve. (Keep the valve for other projects.) You need about 3 feet (1 meter) of tube for this launcher. Stretch one end over the end of the piece of PVC and tape it in place (4 inches, or 10 centimeters, of duct tape). Stretch the other end over the mouth of a 2-liter bottle and use masking tape to hold it in place. You're ready to launch.

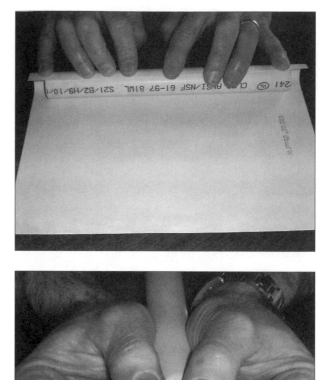

5. Slide your rocket onto the PVC pipe. Aiming the rocket in a safe direction, stomp in the middle of the 2-liter bottle.

6. The rocket will fly so fast that you will find it difficult to follow it. But, it will travel only a few meters. It will twist in mid-flight and quickly lose energy, falling to the ground. The challenge in this activity is to get the rocket to fly far—much farther.

7. To recharge the launcher, blow hard into the PVC pipe. This will re-inflate the bottle, which will be good for 40 to 50 launches, provided that you don't stomp on the end of the bottle. If several people are going to be re-inflating the launcher, use some antibacterial wipes to clean the pipe. There are several things that you can do to get a longer range:

• Add fins. Use index cards to cut one or more fins. Students often make two mistakes when adding fins. They make them much bigger than they need to be, thus slowing down the rocket by giving it more drag. Or, they place the fins in the middle of the rocket, where wings would go on a plane. Fins provide directional stability through drag; they slow the back of the rocket to keep it behind the front of the rocket. To get great distance (more than 120 feet, or 36 meters), you need the smallest fins that provide directional guidance. Determining the optimal size of fins is an engineering exercise that is a great learning experience.

• Add a nose cone. Roll a sized piece of paper into a cone and tape it onto the top of the rocket. A symmetric nose cone will add a few meters to your rocket.

• Add weight. This seems counterintuitive, but adding a few paper clips will usually increase the range of a rocket. Kids can keep adding paper clips until their rocket doesn't go farther. This is another introduction to engineering, where good design requires a balance between conflicting effects. Too much weight will ground the rocket and not enough will cause it to run out of energy in mid-flight.

continued on next page ➤

Pneumatic-blast Rockets (continued)

As teams improve their rockets, have them record their rocket's name and the distance it flies on the blackboard. This will motivate everyone to work harder. In this simple activity they experience a scientific investigation. They build models and test them. They observe and relate their observation to physical features on the rocket. They make changes and repeat the experiment.

Learning Moments

For best overall results, have the class work in teams of two or three. Show them how to make a rocket, but don't mention fins, weights, or nose cones. Let them come up with ideas for these. Challenge them to add design elements to their rockets so they fly far.

As they launch their rocket the first few times, ask each team:

• "What did your rocket do?" If they don't know, have them repeat the launch, knowing that you will ask the same question again.

• "Why did your rocket do what it did?" Have them look at their rocket to see what feature might have caused the effect they saw. Emphasize that design features cause flight effects.

• "What one feature will you change?" Change only one variable at a time and record what the impact of that change is. This is how science moves forward. Changing two or more variables at once will mean you won't know which one was responsible for the impact and you won't know which one you should change further.

• After addressing your questions, send them to make the one change and to try their rocket again.

This basic launcher works well, but it doesn't allow you to measure angles of launch, and it requires you to kneel on the ground during launches. A better launcher involves an hour of work. Use a 2-x-4-inch (5-x-10-centimeter) board or other material to build a foot that can support a 4-foot-long (1.2-meter-long) pine board vertically. Mount a protractor (or a photocopy of a protractor) on the upper end of the launcher. Drill a hole through the center of the protractor that the 2-inch-long (5-centimeter-long) bolt can fit through. Drill a hole through the 2.5-inch (6-centimeter) PVC pipe so you can bolt the pipe to the board. Hot-glue the launch tube (3/4-inch, or 2-centimeter, PVC, 10 inches, or 25 centimeters, long) on the inside of the larger PVC pipe. Bolt the larger diameter PVC pipe to the board and secure with two nuts or a wing nut. Now, you can adjust and measure the angle of launch.

By adding a protractor to the launcher, students can measure the launch angle and compare it to the distance rockets travel. They can graph this set of data (fourth grade and above) and explain what the graph shows. As an incentive to draw the graph, promise that they can try to launch their rocket over the school or some large object at whatever angle they want, based on their graphs.

Rocket-powered History:

Rocket Man

Robert Goddard was the rocket man. He started work on rockets in 1899 when he was seventeen years old. At the time people didn't think rockets could fly in space. He proved them wrong.

Goddard developed solid-fueled rockets and devices to control the flight of rockets. He was also the first person to launch a liquid fuel rocket. In the course of his research, he was awarded more than 200 patents for his inventions. In an era when few people believed in Goddard or his work, he kept working and helped launch the age of space exploration.

Chapter 4

Powered by Pumps

Rockets move as they release fluids contained under pressure inside. Space rockets burn fuel, and this combustion releases the energy to propel them. Hot, expanding gases escape from the back of the rocket and push the rocket forward.

Safer and easier to use in the classroom is the approach of using pumps to raise the pressure of air and to store the compressed air in containers. Water rockets, which are often used in scholastic science events, are powered by air pressure. Increasing the pressure inside the rocket by pumping transforms muscular energy into pressure. When the rocket is launched, the air pressure is released, and the escaping air and water push the rocket upward.

Science stores sell an inexpensive version of the water rocket made of plastic. The pump that comes with a toy water rocket sucks in air through the small hole in the back of the pump. Pushing the handle inward compresses the air, raising the pressure. This pushes a steel ball up inside the valve, letting air escape the pump and flow into the rocket. Increasing pressure in the rocket eventually limits how much air can be forced in. Pulling back on the catch releases the rocket. The rocket flies because the pressure inside forces water and air out the opening. The downward force of the water pushes the rocket upward.

What role does the water play in these water rockets? Try firing a water rocket without water. It will barely lift off. Completely fill the rocket, with water leaving no room for air, will give a similar result. Thus, there is some optimum level of water. Air pushes the water out of the rocket, but it is the water (which has a thousand times more mass per volume than air) that provides the change in momentum (mass times velocity) that propels the rocket.

So if escaping water is what propels the rocket, why do you need air? Water is incompressible; you can't squeeze it into a smaller volume. No matter how hard you pump, you won't get more water into the rocket once it's full. Air, on the other hand, is highly compressible. So you can squeeze more and more into the rocket, building the pressure inside the rocket to push out the water.

Try This:
Potato Rockets

The simplest pump compresses a fluid and operates without valves. To demonstrate compression and the work it can do, launch a spud.

Materials

- Potatoes
- Electrical conduit tubing (EMT)
- 1/2-inch-diameter (1.25-centimeter) dowel

Hardware stores carry electrical conduit (EMT). You can purchase it in lengths of 8 feet (2.4 meters) and cut it with a hacksaw, or ask the store to cut it for you.

Procedure

1. Use a length of pipe that is an inch shorter than the dowel. A 3- to 4-foot (1- to 1.3-meter) length is good. Hold a potato on top of one end of the tubing, with the other end of the tubing on a hard surface. Whack the potato onto and into the pipe with the flat of your hand. A few whacks will force a piece of the potato into the pipe. When the pipe comes through the potato, stop. Pull the potato, now with a cylindrical hole punched through it, off the pipe. Turn the pipe upside-down and repeat the procedure.

2. A cylinder of potato should now be wedged in each end of the pipe. Force one cylinder a bit farther into the pipe using the dowel. Hold the dowel, now barely sticking into one end of the pipe, and the pipe in one hand, and invert the apparatus. Now rest the dowel on the ground. To hold the base of the dowel in place, put it against the instep of one foot.

3. Grab the pipe with your other hand. Aiming the pipe at a 45-degree angle elevation and away from people and breakable stuff, pull the pipe downward as quickly as possible. With a resounding "kurwop," the potato rocket will fly 30 to 50 feet (9 to 15 meters). You launched the piece of potato that was in the upper end of the pipe. The piece of potato in the lower end of the tubing, which serves as wadding, fell limply. Repeat launching the potato until it is consumed with holes.

Explanation

You've demonstrated a simple pump. The potatoes make an almost airtight seal, trapping the air molecules inside—between the two pieces. By pushing the bottom cylinder of potato upward with the dowel, you compressed the air inside the tube. Decreasing the volume increased the pressure. (That's Boyle's Law—pressure times volume is a constant, given that temperature is constant. So as the volume decreases, the pressure increases.) As the dowel and bottom potato moved upward, air pressure inside the tubing increased. Eventually, the force of air pressure exceeded the frictional forces holding the upper potato in place, and out it came.

An air pump compresses air, forcing the molecules closer together and raising the pressure. It converts mechanical energy (a person working to operate the pump or a motor) into higher pressure and heat. (Feel a bike pump after you've filled a tire and you'll notice it is hotter than it was before pumping.) Pushing down the handle of a bike pump forces the air inside into a smaller volume at the distant end. The raised pressure opens a valve letting the air escape into the inner tube or basketball, provided that the pressure is higher than the pressure inside the tube or ball. The valve stem in an inner tube lets air at higher pressure in and prevents air from escaping.

On the return stroke, pulling up on the pump handle reduces the pressure and that allows a valve in the pump to open so more air can enter. In this type of pump system, there are two valves: one letting air out of the pump into the tire or ball, and one letting air into the pump. There are other types of pumps for compressing or moving other fluids; David Macaulay's book, *The Way Things Work*, gives explanations and illustrations.

Try This:
Take Apart a Pump

Materials

- Discarded hand pump from a container of hand cream or liquid soap
- Pocket knife
- Pair of pliers
- Food coloring
- Water

IMPORTANT SAFETY NOTE

This activity involves cutting with a knife and so requires adult supervision.

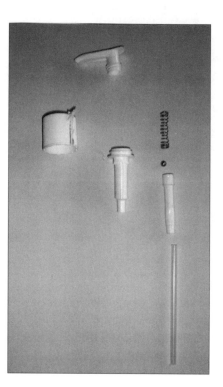

Procedure

1. Remove the pump from the bottle and rinse it to get rid of any of the product. To see how it works, mix a few drops of a dark food color in a glass of water. Hold the pump's tube in the colored water and depress the pump once.

2. Nothing happens when you press on the handle, but when you release it, the colored water moves up the tube. However, nothing comes out the end. Pump it again to see the water rise farther up the tube. Now you have pumped water up to the top of the pump, and when you push on the handle again, colored water squirts out.

3. That's not the experiment. That was getting ready to do the experiment. When you are ready to cut open the pump, ask the class what they expect to find inside and write their ideas on the board. When a few ideas have been expressed, start cutting. (Of course, you could do all the cutting in advance and show the parts to the class. But, that would not be nearly as interesting as seeing you take it apart.)

4. The hardest part is cutting away the plastic collar that attaches the pump to the plastic bottle. Cut through one side of the collar and break it open with the pliers. The collar doesn't contribute to the pumping action, so it doesn't matter if you destroy it. Try pumping the colored water again to see that the pump still works without the collar.

5. Pull off the handle. Yank upward; it requires a good tug to free it. It is hollow so the hand cream or soap can travel through it and out the exit hole.

6. Pull off the plastic tube that extended into the bottom of the bottle. It is held in place by friction, so it comes off easily.

7. Use pliers to extract the plastic plunger that was attached to the handle. This can be hard to do, but keep tugging. When it is out of the way, look inside the tube to see if you find what you thought would be there.

Explanation

Now you can get a good idea of how the pump works. When you press on the handle, it pushes on the plunger and it compresses the spring. The steel ball sits at the bottom of the pump. Nothing happens. The steel ball covers the hole and stops air or liquids from going down the tube.

When you release the handle, the spring pushes it and the plunger back up. The reduced pressure inside the plastic housing draws some of the water (or liquid product) up the tube. Stated differently, atmospheric pressure presses the water into the tube when there is lower pressure inside the tube. The steel ball slides out of the way to let the liquid enter the chamber and then falls back to the bottom. When you press again on the handle, the steel ball prevents the liquid in the chamber from escaping back to the bottle. But because there is less room in the chamber, the liquid has to go somewhere. It goes up the center of the plunger and out the hole in the handle.

You have just reverse-engineered a pump and found out how engineers design things to blow liquid products out of containers. Compare the findings to the predictions. Scientists are often wrong in their predictions. What's important is that the experience leads to better understanding.

Rocket-powered Application:

Water Pistols

Water pistols are pumps too. Pushing the trigger pumps water into the two white tubes that squirt it out. The best water pistols for disassembly are those held together with just a few screws.

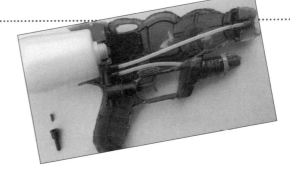

Model To Make:
Rocket on a String

You've probably launched a balloon on a string; a rocket on a string is the same idea but with higher pressure and a rigid rocket. You can store quite a bit of pressure in a small plastic bottle, enough to propel the bottle impressively. The two problems to overcome are how to control the path of the rocket and how to pressurize it and release it.

Materials

- Nylon string
- 1-liter water bottles with caps
- Drill and bits
- Bike pump with pressure gauge
- Inflating needle (used for basketballs/footballs)
- Straws
- Silly Putty®
- Safety glasses

IMPORTANT SAFETY NOTE ⚠️
This activity requires the use of safety goggles by all participants.

Procedure

1. Making the rocket is easy. Drill a hole in the lid of a 1-liter soda bottle. Use a drill bit that will just barely admit the inflating needle. To size the drill bit, do a test on a scrap of wood. Hold the lid in a vice while drilling. After drilling, screw the lid back on the bottle.

2. This rocket can fly far, so make the test range at least 50 feet (15 meters) or even farther. Secure one end of string to an immovable object. Before tying the other end to an equally immovable object, thread the string through a straw. Then, use a cinch knot to tension the string as much as you can and secure it.

3. Tape the rocket to the straw, making sure it is aligned with its long axis parallel to the string. If the nozzle is pointing away from the axis of the string, the rocket will spin around the string rather than traveling far. Which way should the cap be facing? Make sure that everyone agrees that the bottom of the bottle (not the cap) should be facing toward the long expanse of the string.

Explanation

Unlike the pneumatic-blast rocket, this is a true rocket. Gases under pressure inside the rocket exhaust from the rear of the rocket to propel it forward. The string provides the guidance system, keeping the rocket traveling in the desired direction.

4. Wrap a gob of Silly Putty around the base of the inflating needle. With the needle attached to the pump hose, insert it into the opening in the bottle. Press the needle against the cap, compressing the Silly Putty to make a good seal. Have someone pump while you hold the needle; you will need to hold the bottle in one hand and the inflating needle in the other.

5. At some pressure (probably around 40 PSI) the seal will fail and air will escape as fast as it is pumped into the rocket. You'll hear a "pop" and the hiss of escaping air, and this will clue you to release the rocket.

6. Kids could test their rockets at different pump pressures, with and without fins (or air brakes/parachutes), and with different-sized bottles and see how far they travel. Because of the variability of each launch, students will need to conduct several tests at each pressure and average the distances traveled. With good control of the launch pressure, students could collect enough data to warrant graphing pressure vs. distance.

Model To Make:

Rocket Cars

This model uses the same approach to storing and releasing energy as does the "Rocket on a String" activity. However, it provides the additional challenge of designing and building a car chassis and aligning the wheels so the car travels in a straight line. Students can work in teams of two or three.

Materials

- 1-liter water bottles with caps
- Drill and bits
- Bike pump with pressure gage
- Inflating needle (used for basketballs/footballs)
- Silly Putty
- 2-inch (5-centimeter) wood wheels (available from www.craftparts.com)
- 1/4-inch (.6-centimeter) dowels (available from www.craftparts.com)
- "Fat" straws
- Cardboard
- Scissors
- Hot-glue gun
- Coping saws
- Masking tape
- Scissors

Procedure

1. Students cut chassis from cardboard boxes and glue pieces of "fat" straw to the bottom, making sure that they are parallel to each other. They cut axles (from dowels) long enough to pass through the straws with room enough to attach wheels. It is easier to connect one wheel to each axle, slide the axles through the straws, and then attach the second wheel. Of course, they don't have to use two wheels per axle. Some could try one wheel per axle or more than two wheels.

2. Before adding the engine (water bottle), they should test their cars. With a push, does the car roll far? If not, the wheels might be rubbing on the chassis or the axles might be rubbing on the straws. Does it travel in a straight line? It's easier to fix these problems now, before working on the propulsion.

3. They can tape or glue the bottle to the chassis. The challenge is to get the bottle aligned with the direction that car will travel. If it is pointed off to one side, the car will spin around, doing wheelies.

4. You or they can drill holes in the lids. They screw on the lids and are ready for testing.

5. The floor surface has a lot to do with the success of these cars. Too slippery, and the cars can easily veer out of control. Too much friction, and the cars won't go far. Try the different surfaces available to see which works best.

6. Mark the start line with a piece of masking tape. You might mark intervals along the intended direction of travel to make measuring easier and quicker, but have each team of students measure the distance traveled for each run—measuring either from the start line or from the interval markers you established.

7. Have teams try to maximize the range of their cars. Encourage them to innovate new designs and solve each new technical problem. Later, have them report how they were able to get their cars go far.

When each team has had the chance to test and improve their cars, have them test the cars at different air pressures. They will need to test them at least three times at each pressure and average the distances, starting at 5 PSI and going in 5-PSI increments to the highest pressure they can obtain (probably 40 PSI).

Learning Moments

As teams line up to launch their rocket cars, ask them what direction their car will travel and what direction the escaping air will travel. They should know that the car would travel in the direction opposite to its airflow. This gives you an opportunity to state Newton's Second Law of Motion: If the car nozzle directs the air backward, the air pushes the car forward.

Model To Make:

Water Rockets

On a warm day, water rockets are the best way to learn science. Every launch elicits "Ahs" and "That's neat," and the spray of water cools the launchers. Just watching and understanding what happens is a great experience. Even better is to engage in the challenge of keeping your rocket in the air for the longest time.

These rockets demonstrate Newton's Third Law of Motion. Rockets are propelled by ejecting mass out the back. The forward force is the reaction to this backward force. The force is proportional to the exhaust velocity multiplied by the rate that mass is ejected. Water, which has a mass density 1,000 times larger than air, provides the high mass required for large thrust. Air, which is highly compressible, provides the mechanism for storing energy (pressure) and pushing out the water. Getting the right proportion of water to air is critical to achieving the highest launches.

Materials

- 2-liter bottles
- Bike pump with pressure gauge
- Launcher
- Water
- Stopwatch
- Cardboard (cereal boxes)
- Duct tape
- Scissors
- Safety glasses

You can make a very durable launcher from components found at a hardware store and using plans found in *Fantastic Flying Fun with Science* by Ed Sobey (see the References at the end of this book). Or, you can purchase a launcher from a science supply house, such as The Science Source (www.sciencesource.com), at very low cost.

Empty 2-liter bottles are the standard for the rocket, but you can also use smaller bottles. These bottles appear to be safe up to pressures of about 125 PSI, but it is a good idea not to inflate them higher than 80 PSI. 60 PSI sends a rocket impressively high, so you might use that as an upper limit.

IMPORTANT SAFETY NOTE ⚠

This activity requires the use of safety goggles by all participants.

Procedure

1. A bare bottle will fly high but will tumble. To get it flying higher, add fins, a nose cone, and weight. To keep it in the air longer, add a parachute. Students can cut fins from empty cereal boxes and duct-tape them onto the rockets. The larger the fins are, the more control and drag they provide. The engineering challenge is to minimize the drag while getting enough control. Fins set at a uniform angle to the rocket will cause it to spiral (roll), like a football. Such fins add drag (deflect air) but can help stabilize the direction of flight.

2. Although counterintuitive, adding weight helps a rocket go higher. An easy way to add weight is to tape a small, water-filled balloon to the top of the rocket. Plastic bags make good parachutes. The trick is how to attach a parachute so it deploys as the rocket is coming down (and not when it is going up). It will take some experimentation to develop the right technique.

3. Pour some water into an empty bottle. We recommend filling a bottle about 1/4 to 1/3 full. Then set the rocket on the launcher.

⚠ IMPORTANT SAFETY NOTE

It takes discipline to safely launch water rockets with a group of students. They must stay at least 10 feet (3.3 meters) back from the launcher and be sitting on the ground, not standing up. There can be no messing around. Launching occurs only when you give the command, assured that everyone is in a safe position. The person operating the pump must heed the upper pressure limit.

4. With a rocket mounted on the launcher, have one person sit on the ground ready to pull on the launch lanyard. Another stands by the pump. At your signal the pumper begins, calling out pressures every 10 PSI. When the specified limit is reached, have the pumper step back and then have the launcher pull.

5. Occasionally, a misfire will occur. The rocket could be off-center on the launcher or the seal between the bottle and the inflating hose might have slipped. Doing nothing will let the pressure escape, allowing you to re-set the rocket and try again.

6. To demonstrate the role that water plays, do two tests after having launched a few rockets. Launch one bottle that is completely full of water. It won't go very high, probably not more than 10 feet (3.3 meters). Then try one that has no water; it will go higher, but not nearly as high as rockets partially filled with water.

7. You can test for the height of launches or for the time in the air. Estimating the height is tricky. A rough measurement would be to launch in front of a tall building and comparing the rocket's apogee to some mark on the building. This will give you a four-story measurement or a three-story measurement. Use a stopwatch for measuring time. Without parachutes rockets will stay in the air for about the same period, which makes precisely starting and stopping the watch critical.

continued on next page ➤

Water Rockets (continued)

8. Students can measure the height or time aloft as they vary any of several factors. Height vs. pressure is the first to explore. The quantity of water is another. With a scale, they could compare weight added (water balloon weight) to height. They could also measure the surface area of uniformly shaped fins. There are many different science fair projects or class projects that involve experiment design, data collection and analysis, graphing, and reporting, and kids will love to do them.

Explanation

This is a true rocket. Pressurized air forces the water out of the mouth of the bottle. The force propelling the rocket upward is related to the time rate of change of the mass being ejected. The larger the mass (which is why water is used and not just air) and the faster it is ejected (due to higher pressure), the higher the rocket will fly.

Learning Moments

One phenomenon to note is the formation of fog inside the rocket bottles. Under pressure, water is vaporized inside the bottle. Upon launching, the pressure inside rapidly drops and the water vapor condenses into droplets—fog. By squeezing a launched bottle you can force puffs of fog out of the bottle. Have students think about where the fog comes from or how it forms.

As a student operates the pump, ask him where the energy comes from that flies the rocket. It should be obvious to this worker that he is supplying the energy. Continue by asking where he got the energy and by pointing out that nearly everything on our planet gets it energy (ultimately) from the sun.

Model To Make:
Pump Rockets

People love to make and launch rockets, and this launcher is perfect for a large, indoor space. Pump rockets take the same form as in pneumatic-blast rockets, except pump rockets use a smaller-diameter launch tube and rocket fuselage. To launch these, kids push down on the handle of a pump.

Although it takes longer to build and is more expensive than the pneumatic-blast rocket, the pump rocket offers some advantages. You don't need to collect 2-liter bottles and you don't have to inflate the bottle between each launch. For one group of students, the pneumatic-blast launcher is the way to go, but for a larger group or a continuous flow of people (say, a science day celebration or a permanent activity in a science museum), the pump launcher is a better choice.

Materials

For the rocket:

Refer to the Pneumatic-blast Rocket activity on page 63 for materials and directions on how to make the rockets. This rocket differs in that you wrap the paper around a smaller pipe—in this case, 1/2-inch-diameter (1.25-centimeter) CPVC. Students can try using a full sheet of plain white paper or a partial sheet (1/4, 1/3, or 1/2 sheet). As with the pneumatic-blast rocket, students add fins, weight, and a nose cone.

For the launcher:

- 2-foot-x-2-foot (0.6-meter-x-0.6-meter) sheet of 5/8-inch or 3/4-inch plywood for the base
- 2 x 4 (stud) to lift the base off the ground, 8 feet (2.4 meters) long
- 1-inch-x-10-inch (2.5-centimeter-x-25-centimeter) pine board for the plunger and launch tower, 6 feet (1.8 meters) long
- 1/2-inch CPVC pipe, 8 feet (2.4 meters) long
- 2-inch PVC pipe, 4 inches (10 centimeters) long

- Vinyl tubing 5/8-inch ID, 3/4-inch OD, 4 feet
- Plastic fitting for vinyl tube (see photo above)
- 4-inch-diameter ABS sewer pipe, 20 inches (50 centimeters) long
- 4-inch end cap for the ABS pipe
- 4-inch hole saw
- 3/4-inch-diameter PVC pipe, schedule 40, 30 inches (75 centimeters) long
- 3/4-inch-diameter PVC pipe end caps (flat), 3 of them
- 3/4-inch-diameter PVC pipe "T"
- Rubber shelf liner (comes in rolls)
- Shelf brackets to support the launch tower
- Drill and bits
- Protractor
- PVC cement
- Bolts, nuts, and screws
- Stapling gun
- Safety glasses

<table>
<tr><td>⚠️</td></tr>
<tr><td>IMPORTANT SAFETY NOTE</td></tr>
<tr><td>This activity requires adult supervision and the use of safety goggles.</td></tr>
</table>

Pump Rockets (continued)

Building the Launcher

The launcher requires working with wood and spending some time in a hardware store scratching your head. If, after reading the directions for building the launcher, your head is spinning, go to Kelvin.com for a comparable, slightly smaller, launcher.

The launcher is a large pump made from a 4-inch (10-centimeter) ABS sewer pipe. Hardware stores sell these in short lengths and you need a 20-inch (50-centimeter) length. You will anchor this pipe to a wood base so the pipe stands vertically.

The plunger mechanism is cut out of a piece of pine board using a 4-inch hole or circle saw on a high-speed drill. Use 3/4-inch-diameter (0.625-centimeter-diameter) PVC for the handle.

1. Construct a base by screwing lengths of 2 x 4 lumber into the edge of the plywood sheet. This will elevate the base and make it easier to attach the launch tube.

2. Cut two 4-inch-diameter (10-centimeter-diameter) circles from the end of the pine board. Screw one into one end of the ABS sewer tube. Bolt the launch tube through the wood circle into the center of the base.

3. Cut a hole for the plastic fitting and screw it in place.

4. Bolt the second 4-inch-diameter (10-centimeter-diameter) wood circle to a flat end cap (3/4-inch-diameter, or 0.625-centimeter-diameter PVC). The end cap fits onto a 24-inch (60-centimeter) length of PVC pipe. You can hold the end cap on the PVC pipe either with PVC cement or with a small screw. Using a screw will make it possible to make repairs to the plunger.

5. Drill a hole through the ABS end cap that allows the PVC pipe to slide through. Slide the plunger into the launch tube and fit the ABS end cap on the top of the tube. Add the PVC "T" to the top of the PVC pipe. Insert two 4-inch (10-centimeter) lengths of pipe into the "T" for handles and add PVC caps to the ends.

6. The launch tower gets the fast-moving rockets up away from eyes and allows you to set the angle of the launch. Use shelf brackets to attach the remaining part of the pine board onto the base. Glue a protractor to the top of the board and drill a 5/16-inch-diameter hole through the center of the protractor's base. Bolt the short section of 2-inch (5-centimeter) PVC pipe through this hole. Glue an 18-inch (46-centimeter)length of the CPVC pipe to the inside of the PVC pipe so one end of the CPVC pipe extends about 4 inches (10 centimeters). Connect the vinyl tubing to the short end of the CPVC pipe. You're ready to test.

7. You may find that your launcher works great without further work. If, however, it doesn't develop enough compression, cut gaskets from rubber shelf liner. First try a gasket for the bottom of the wood circle plunger. Glue a piece of rubber in place and cut it so it extends a bit beyond the edge of the wood circle. If this doesn't seal well enough, cut a 3/4-inch-wide (0.625-centimeter-wide) strip of the rubber and glue it to the edge of the wood plunger. Hold it in place with staples and rubber bands.

Procedure

Show students how to create a fuselage by rolling paper around a 12-inch (30-centimeter) length of the CPVC pipe. Let them figure out how to add fins, weight, and nose cones from paper, index cards, and paper clips. They need to experience launching their rockets a few times to understand how best to push the handle—a slow, long stroke or a fast, short stroke. Once they have mastered the art of launching, have them focus on learning through experimenting.

Have them measure and record their launch distances along with the launch angle. Insist that they make one change to their rocket between each test. That is, if they are adding fins, insist that they don't also change the launch angle until they have made at least one test at the previously used launch angle.

Encourage teams to share information with each other on what works well and what doesn't work at all. Although teams and individuals will be vying to create the rocket that flies farthest, they should understand that the rocket launch is a scientific inquiry in which the goal is for everyone to learn and help each other learn.

Chapter 5

Implosions and Explosions Even Your Mother Will Like

Dynamite! That's probably what comes to mind when you think of blowing up stuff. You might think of other types of explosions too, such as the hundreds of explosions occurring each second inside your car's engine or the explosion of a firecracker.

Chemical explosions occur when chemicals are added to each other or heat is applied to a material to start a chemical reaction. What is unique about explosives is that they burn or react quickly. The reaction gives off heat and a gas. The gas takes up much more space than did the original chemicals and forms a pressure wave that radiates in all directions at the speed of sound.

One of the most powerful explosives is nitroglycerin (pronounced "ny truh GLIHS uhr ihn"). When it explodes, the hot gases generated take up 3,000 times as much space as the unexploded nitroglycerin did. Usually nitroglycerin is mixed with other materials to make it safer to handle.

Now let's look at some implosions and explosions you and your students can try safely.

Rocket-powered History:

The Dynamite Prize

Imagine being a neighbor of Alfred Nobel. If you had lived close to him you would have thought of him as a mad and dangerous scientist. Nobel studied how to blow up things safely. Ascanio Sobrero invented nitroglycerin in 1846, but few people used it because it was too dangerous. You couldn't always tell when it would explode. Nobel wanted to find a way to use nitroglycerin safely.

As he experimented with different chemicals, Nobel created a lot of explosions. Some were planned and some were accidents. People thought he was dangerous because he was always blowing up things. But after he invented dynamite in 1867, which made explosions much safer, Nobel gained respect—and money.

Dynamite made Nobel rich. Dynamite helped people solve problems in mining and construction, and they bought lots of it. We might say that Alfred Nobel was the father of safe blow-ups.

Some people used dynamite to hurt others and that disturbed Nobel. So he set aside $9 million of his earnings to give awards each year to honor scientific discoveries and inventions and great writing and to promote world peace. The annual awards, the Nobel prizes, are for accomplishments in physics, chemistry, physiology or medicine, literature, and peace. A sixth prize, for the study of economics, was added in 1969. Nobel not only gave the world a great invention; he used his profits from that invention to recognize the great accomplishments of others.

Try This:
Explode a Straw

There is nothing like hands-on experience to help understand a subject—say, for instance, explosions. Explosions are sudden releases of pressure that we experience through sound and shock waves that you can feel. This activity helps students understand what an explosion is.

Materials

- Straws

Procedure

1. Grab the straw at each end by holding it between your thumbs and forefingers. Roll your hands in a circle to get the straw to pinch itself. Don't let it wrap around your fingers. Make three or four circles with your hands, leaving 1 inch or so (2 to 3 centimeters) of the straw left untwisted.

2. Have someone flick the straw as hard as he or she can to make it explode. To get a great flick, have the student hold a forefinger against a thumb and press hard. Then, as fast as the flicker can, he or she lets the forefinger fly into the straw. Kaboom!

3. If the straw doesn't explode, either the flicker didn't flick hard enough, or the straw holder, that's you, let air out of the straw. First, ask another student to try flicking the straw. If that doesn't bring a satisfying sound, try a new straw. Make sure you wrap the straw tightly around itself and then call in the new flicker.

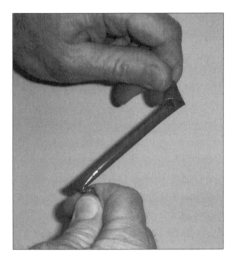

Explanation

The result of this experiment is that you got a neat-sounding explosion. Look for the hole in the straw where it burst. All the air you trapped inside the straw came out here and the sudden release of air created a sound wave. Kaboom!

The trick to exploding the straw is building up the pressure inside the straw so a flick will rupture it. When you started twisting the straw, you sealed the ends so the air inside couldn't escape. With each additional twist, you compressed the air inside the straw, forcing it into the smaller space in the middle. By compressing the air in the straw, you raise its *pressure*, which is the force per area.

continued on next page ➤

Explode a Straw *(continued)*

Think about pressure for a second. If you were wearing snowshoes, you could walk on fresh powder snow. Your weight would be spread over a large area so the pressure, or weight per area, was low enough so you didn't sink deep into the snow. Take off the snowshoes and stand on a pogo stick, with all your weight concentrated on a small area, and you'd sink through the snow. In each case your weight (the force) was the same, but the pressure you exerted was different.

In the exploding straw you forced more air into a small space and all those molecules of air pushed against the side of the straw increasing the pressure. The sudden flick quickly raised the pressure to the point at which it exceeded the strength of the straw. You heard the escaping air as an explosion.

Another type of explosion occurs when you use the engine in a car or bus. In your car's engine, gasoline is mixed with air and compressed by the piston. A spark from the spark plug explodes the mixture, which releases heat and gas. The explosion drives the piston down and as it moves, the piston turns the crankshaft. From there the power is transferred to the driving wheels, and down the highway you go.

Rocket-powered Applications:

Air Bags

Here's an explosion that can protect you in an accident: the air bag in your car. Today most cars come equipped with airbags that blow up to protect you in case of a collision. Ask kids if they know what a car's air bag is and what it does. See if they know where the air is stored that will inflate the bag if you're in an accident. Can they find a tank of compressed air under the hood?

That's a trick question, because the air isn't stored. When sensors in your car detect a collision (a very rapid deceleration or change of speed) they send an electric pulse to a device that explodes. The device explodes a chemical, sodium azide, which releases nitrogen gas. The nitrogen fills the air bag that pops out of the steering wheel or dashboard to protect you from the collision. All that occurs in less than 0.05 seconds.

A fraction of a second after it has filled, the bag deflates. It happens so quickly that people don't have time to see it. Now, that's a fast blow-up!

The bag spreads the force of the collision over a larger area, so you are less likely to bump your head or chest and sustain an injury. Even with air bags, you need to wear seat belts.

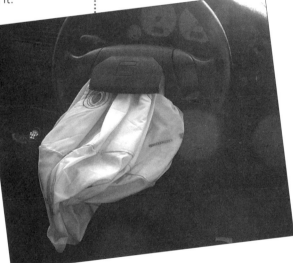

Try This:
Party Poppers

These are safe explosive devices used as party favors. Yank on the string to cause a loud explosion and a shower of paper streamers.

Materials

- Party poppers, available at party stores
- Safety glasses

IMPORTANT SAFETY NOTE ⚠️

This activity requires that you wear safety goggles.

Procedure

1. Hold up a party popper to see if students recognize what it is. Ask them how it works. What causes the large pop and the streamers to fly out?

2. After putting on your safety goggles, aim the popper away from people. Hold the base in one hand and the string in the other.

3. Give the string a sharp yank, and watch the popper explode!

Explanation

The mouth of the popper is covered with a circle of cardboard that holds the streamers inside. A second cardboard circle inside forms the other boundary for the streamers. Beneath the second circle is a small charge of explosives that is ignited by the friction of being pulled through the tiny opening with the string.

The tiny amount of explosives in a party popper is able to launch several streamers and produce a bang heard throughout a large room. If you buy a party popper, be sure to use it safely by pointing it away from yourself and other people.

Try This:
Carbide Cannons

Carbide cannons are popular noise makers sold in hobby stores and through magazine and Internet ads. Calcium carbide, a compound of carbon and calcium, is mixed with water to form acetylene gas which is very explosive. A spark ignites the gas, producing a resounding "wahoomph!"

Materials

- Carbide cannon
- Calcium carbide
- Water
- Safety glasses

IMPORTANT SAFETY NOTE ⚠
This activity requires that you wear safety goggles.

Procedure

Follow the directions that come with the cannon. Do not fire the cannon indoors. Wear safety goggles and keep everyone away from the cannon. The noise is very loud.

Explanation

Mixing the calcium carbide with water causes a chemical reaction that forms calcium hydroxide, $CA(OH)_2$, and acetylene gas (C_2H_2). A spark causes a second reason, the oxidization of the acetylene, that results in carbon dioxide (CO_2) and water (H_2O) and a large release of energy—an explosion. The white precipitate is calcium carbonate ($CaCO_3$)—the same material used as an antacid. It forms when the calcium hydroxide combines with carbon dioxide.

A similar reaction occurs in internal combustion engines where a fuel (gasoline or diesel is mixed with oxygen (about 20 percent of air is oxygen). A spark or pressure powers the reaction that drives the engine.

Rocket-powered Applications:

Explosives at Home

Luckily for us there aren't many things at home that could combine to explode. However, there is one pair of chemicals in your kitchen that react quickly to give an explosive launch to a rocket: vinegar and baking soda.

Try This:
Baking Soda Rockets

Materials

- Vinegar
- Baking soda
- 1-pint plastic container with snap-on lid
- Facial tissue
- Safety glasses

⚠ IMPORTANT SAFETY NOTE
This activity requires the use of safety goggles by all participants.

Procedure

1. Do this experiment either outside or in a sink where clean-up will be easy. Pour a half-cup (125 cubic centimeters) of vinegar into the plastic container. Dump two heaping teaspoons of baking soda onto a tissue and fold the tissue over to hold the soda. The tissue slows down the reaction so you have time to get the lid on the container.

2. When you are ready to seal the lid on the container, drop in the tissue packet with baking soda. Finish sealing the container (quickly!) and stand back.

Explanation

Kabomb! It took a few seconds for the chemical reaction to produce enough gas to blow the lid off. The reaction continued, making more gas, and if you are fast enough you might get the lid back on for a second try.

Vinegar is an acid and baking soda is a base. When mixed, they react with each other to produce a gas, carbon dioxide. Bakers use this chemical reaction to leaven or blow bubbles into cakes and breads. Without a leavening agent, your birthday cake would be as flat as a pancake.

In the plastic container the reaction took place quickly. The carbon dioxide gas increased the pressure inside the container until the force was greater than the force holding the lid on: "Houston, we have a baking soda-vinegar lift-off!"

Try This:
Film Canister Rockets I

This is a great demonstration with opportunities for experiments. Students will ask you to repeat this demonstration over and over.

Materials

- Clear film canisters
- Alka Seltzer® or its generic equivalent
- Water
- Safety glasses

The film canisters must be ones that have the top clip into the inside of the canister. The black canisters with lids that snap around the outside don't work.

IMPORTANT SAFETY NOTE ⚠️

This activity requires the use of safety goggles by all participants.

Procedure

1. Start on a surface that is happy to get wet, and with lots of overhead room. These rockets can fly 20 feet (6.5 meters) high. Fill the film canister one-third to one-half full of water. If you're not already wearing safety glasses or goggles, put them on now. Students need to see you taking safety precautions so they understand the importance of protecting their eyes.

2. Drop in a third of an antacid tablet and quickly snap on the lid. Invert the canister and stand back.

It takes a few seconds for the rocket to blast off. When it does, it moves so quickly it will be difficult to follow it in flight.

continued on next page ➤

Film Canister Rockets I (continued)

Explanation

The antacid tablet reacts with water to create carbon dioxide gas. Although the liquid (water) and solid (tablet) fit comfortably in the canister, their reaction generated a gas that raised the pressure inside. As more gas was generated and the pressure rose, eventually the force (pressure times surface area) exceeded the frictional forces holding the lid in place. The pressure sent the canister skyward and a pressure wave to your ear: "pop."

Learning Moments

The sudden release of pressure downward launched the rocket upward, against the pull of gravity. Have students explain this in their own words.

Chemical reactions, like vinegar and baking soda or Alka Seltzer and water, result in a change in the materials. In the examples, a liquid and solid combined to make a gas. The molecules of each substance broke apart and their atoms formed a different molecule. Unlike physical reactions, you can't reverse chemical reactions.

Try This:
Implode a Can

Materials

- An empty soda can
- Tongs that will let you hold the can when it is very hot
- Stove or hot plate
- Water
- Sink or basin filled with ice-cold water
- Safety glasses

IMPORTANT SAFETY NOTES
Wear safety goggles at all times during this activity. *This demonstration requires heating water to boiling, so it also requires keeping students a safe distance away.*

Procedure

1. Fill a sink or basin with cold water and toss in two or three handfuls of ice. Let the temperature stabilize for several minutes.

2. Put approximately 2 tablespoons of tap water in the can and place it securely on the stovetop.

3. Turn on the stove to high heat so, in a few minutes, the water inside will boil. When you see water vapor rising out of the can, you know the water is boiling and it's time to implode the can.

4. Engage the class with a question about what is happening. In front of their eyes is a series of energy transfers that define the industrial age. It was steam power that replaced animal and human power, made manufacturing and rapid transportation possible, and changed the world. The heat is raising the water temperature to the boiling point—the temperature can't go above this point (without an increase in pressure, which

is impossible in an open container). That is, the energy level of the water is rising—it is measurable as the water temperature rises. At the boiling point, water molecules are so energetic that some break the attractive bonds of their neighbors, become a gas (water vapor), and escape into the air above the water. The can is now filled with hot gas (water vapor) instead of a gas at room temperature.

As the gas molecules inside gained energy, they moved more rapidly and some left the can through the opening. The hotter, more energetic molecules inside the can took up a greater volume and pushed other molecules out.

You saw "steam" or actually condensed water vapor as the steam encountered cool air outside the can. Where, by the way, did the energy come from to heat the water and convert it into a gas? The heat came from the hot plate, which by now is red hot, giving off energy as light as well as heat. It got hot when the switch was turned on and electrical power traveled through the highly resistive heating coil. Where did the electrical power come from? Check with your local utility, but unless your

continued on next page ➤

Implode a Can *(continued)*

community uses nuclear power, it came from the sun. Sunlight powered the hydrological cycle that put water behind the dam for hydropower and it powered the plants that became coal, oil, and gas.

5. By now, the can will be hot enough and the ice bath cool enough to continue. Pick up the can with tongs, dump the boiling water into a sink (not the one with the cold water), and immediately turn the can upside-down and plunge it into the ice water. Kapomph! The can is history.

Explanation

It happened so fast that it probably startled you. What makes this experiment especially dramatic is that you changed water into steam and back into water. By heating the water in the can so it boiled, you changed it from a liquid to a gas (steam). The gas took up much more room than the liquid did, so it forced its way out of the can, taking air with it. Letting the water boil for a few seconds empties it of most of the air, leaving water and water vapor (steam) inside.

When you dunked the can, now filled with water vapor, into the ice bath, the vapor quickly *condensed*, or changed back to the liquid state. This change reduced the pressure inside the can so much that atmospheric pressure outside collapsed the can. Like we said: "Kapomph!"

So what?

Changing water between liquid and gas states is not just a fun demonstration; it is what drives many engines. Long before gasoline and diesel engines, steam engines were the principal way to get power to do a job. Some cars had steam engines. Today steam engines (turbines) are used in power plants generating electricity, whether fueled with nuclear fuels or fossil fuels. Many ships use steam engines for power.

In steam engines fuel provides the source for heat that boils water into steam. The steam expands and pushes either a turbine or piston that can drive a generator to produce electricity or power wheels or a ship's propeller to give motion. The steam is condensed and fed back into the boiler, where it repeats the cycle.

You can see antique farm steam engines on display at county and state fairs. They hiss and whistle and rock around so you'd think they won't last, but they keep chugging along providing power from steam.

Try This:
Rocket Matches

Match heads ignite quickly and you can use them to make a tiny rocket. Before launching a match, let's think about how it works. To light a safety match, you have to drag the match head across the striking surface. The match head has a chemical that ignites at about 360°F (180°C). When you rub it across the striking surface (made of red phosphorus and sand), the friction generates enough heat to raise the temperature high enough to ignite. The head burns for only a second or so, but during that time ignites the wood or paper stick. The stick requires a temperature higher than 450°F (232°C) to burn. So we ignite the chemicals by generating heat through friction, and they burn hot enough to ignite the wood or paper. All that science happens in lighting a match.

Materials

- Matches
- Paper clip
- Aluminum foil
- Straight pin
- Safety glasses
- Tape

IMPORTANT SAFETY NOTE
This activity involves matches and flame. Make sure all participants are wearing safety glasses, that there is adequate adult supervision, and that the area is cleared of combustibles.

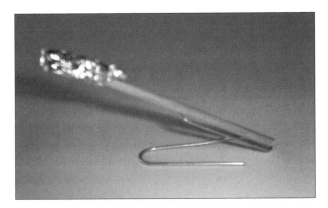

Procedure

The trick to making a rocket out of a match is capturing the hot gases and venting them in the direction opposite to the intended flight. By having the gases vent backward, they will propel the rocket forward, into the air.

1. Cut a piece of aluminum foil about 1 by 1/2 inches (2.5 centimeters by 1.3 centimeters). Place a match on the foil so the head is in the center and the longer dimension of the foil is perpendicular to the match. Lay the pin on top of the match so the sharp end touches the head of the match.

2. Fold the foil over the match, first folding down from the top and then folding around the sides. Compress the foil to eliminate any openings that will let the gases out. Use your thumbnail to crease the foil along the edges of the pin.

3. Slide the pin out backward. This opens up the exhaust channel for the gases.

continued on next page ➤

Rocket Matches (continued)

4. Bend the paper clip into a launcher. Hold the larger loop on a flat surface and pull up on the end of the smaller loop. Tape the larger loop to the surface. Angle the smaller loop about 45 degrees above the surface to give maximum flight.

5. Launch the rocket outside, away from anything that could catch fire. Wear safety glasses or other eye covering.

6. Place the match-rocket on the launch stand with the foil-covered head pointing up. Light a second match and hold it under the foil, ensuring that you and everyone else are out of the way. You will see a small wisp of smoke come out of the vent you made in the aluminum foil, and then "swish," the rocket will take off.

Explanation

You made a chemical rocket. The chemical reaction occurs when the match head burns and this generates heat and gases. The hot gases take up more room and, because they are confined to a small space, pressure builds. The gases vent through the hole where the pin was, so they vent to the rear with enough force to launch the match forward as much as 10 feet (3 meters).

Try some experiments with your match-rocket. Would two vents work better than one? Can you get two matches in one rocket? Does a two-match rocket go farther? How do wooden matches compare to paper matches in their ability to rocket? Does it travel farther if you use a smaller piece of aluminum foil (less weight)? Hey, now you are a rocket scientist!

Model To Make:
Film Canister Rockets II

After demonstrating how film canister rockets work, challenge students to make their own rockets and launch platforms to get the greatest horizontal distance.

Materials

- Clear film canisters
- Alka Seltzer® or its generic equivalent
- Water
- Cardboard
- Scissors
- Tape
- Measuring spoons
- Safety glasses

IMPORTANT SAFETY NOTE ⚠
This activity requires the use of safety goggles by all participants.

Procedure

Teams need to make a launch platform from which they can launch their rockets. Launching their rockets straight up won't give them any significant horizontal distance, so they will need to make a launcher that holds the rocket at an angle. They can make a platform out of cardboard or other material and test it at different angles.

Once they have a launcher that holds the rocket at the optimal angle, they can experiment to find the optimal quantity of water and tablet. They can measure the distance from their launcher to the landing and record the distance along with the quantities of water and tablet they used. Students could add fins and other rocket features in a quest to get longer launches.

Ensure that all participants are wearing safety glasses when experimenting. Separate each team so they aren't launching rockets toward each other.

Learning Moments 💡

Another experiment to try is to launch vertically with the heaviest payload possible. They can tape pennies or washers to the top of the canister and see how many the rocket can lift at least 1 foot (30.5 centimeters) above the table.

A different line of inquiry would be to test how long the reaction takes. Chemical reactions occur at different rates depending on the temperature, so students could time the reaction (starting with the addition of the tablet and ending with liftoff) with water of different temperatures. Hot tap water to ice water makes a wide enough temperature range.

They could also test liquids other than water. Would a carbonated beverage or acidic liquid (vinegar) produce a larger explosion and higher launch?

References

....

Anderson, David F. and Scott Eberhardt. *Understanding Flight.*
New York: McGraw-Hill, 2001.

Bloomfield, Louis. *How Things Work: The Physics of Everyday Life.*
New York: John Wiley & Sons, 1997.

Jargodzki, Christopher P. and Franklin Potter. *Mad about Physics.*
New York: John Wiley & Sons, 2001.

Macaulay, David. *The Way Things Work.*
Boston: Houghton Mifflin, 1988.

Sobey, Ed. *Fantastic Flying Fun with Science.*
New York: McGraw-Hill, 2000.

Sobey, Ed. *Inventing Toys: Kids Having Fun Learning Science.*
Chicago: Zephyr Press, 2002.

Sobey, Ed. *Just Plane Smart.*
New York: McGraw-Hill, 1998.

Sobey, Ed. *Young Inventors at Work.*
Glenview, IL: Good Year Books, 1999.

Websites

Explosion Science

http://muller.lbl.gov/teaching/Physics10/chapters/1-Explosions.htm

http://www.newton.dep.anl.gov/askasci/chem00/chem00033.htm

International Aerospace Hall of Fame

http://www.allstar.fiu.edu/aero/iahf.htm

International Space Hall of Fame

http://www.spacefame.org/inductee.html

Rocket History

http://www.allstar.fiu.edu/aero/Rock_Hist1.html

http://sln.fi.edu/tfi/programs/g-scouts/history.html

http://www.spaceline.org/rockethistory.html

Rocket Science

http://au.encarta.msn.com/encyclopedia_761577900/Rocket_(physics).html

http://dept.physics.upenn.edu/courses/gladney/mathphys/subsubsection3_1_3_3.html

http://liftoff.msfc.nasa.gov/academy/rocket_sci/rocket_sci.html

The X-Prize

http://www.xprize.org/

Water Rockets

http://ourworld.compuserve.com/homepages/pagrosse/h2oRocketIndex.htm

http://www.seeds2learn.com/rocketSoftware.html

Glossary

Aerodynamic whistle   A type of whistle that makes sounds by vibrating air without movement of the whistle itself.

Aerosol   Droplets of a liquid carried by a gas.

Bernoulli effect   Faster-moving air has lower air pressure. Blow across a strip of paper and the paper rises, pulled up by the lower pressure associated with the moving air.

Boyle's Law   Robert Boyle discovered the relationship between the volume of a gas and its pressure. Pressure and volume are inversely related. Increasing the pressure decreases the volume.

Charles's Law   Jacques Charles discovered the relationship between the volume of a gas and its temperature. The law states that the volume of a gas is proportional to its absolute temperature.

Condensation   Water droplets that form when humid air is either cooled or undergoes a drop in pressure. Dew forms on grass when moist air near the ground cools.

Density   The weight of a substance per volume that it occupies. For equal volumes of air and water, the water will weigh more. Water has greater density than air.

Explosion   A violent bursting outward, which occurs when pressure builds very quickly inside an object.

Fuselage   The body of an airplane. Take off the wings, engines, tail, and landing gear, and what's left is fuselage.

Hooke's Law   Robert Hooke discovered that the force required to stretch an elastic body is proportional to the deformation of that body.

Hydraulic   Systems used to move or raise things that use fluids under pressure. Hydraulic lifts are used at gas stations to raise cars.

Implosion   A violent collapse inward, which occurs when pressure is much greater outside a container.

Newton's Laws of Motion   Sir Isaac Newton discovered the three laws of motion that bear his name:

> **First Law of Motion**   Objects moving at a fixed velocity remain at that velocity unless subjected to an external force.

> **Second Law of Motion**   Applying a force to an object causes it to accelerate at a rate dependent upon its mass and in the same direction as the force. $F = ma$, where F is the force, m is the mass, and a is the acceleration.

> **Third Law of Motion**   Every force has an associated reaction that is equal to the measure of the force and in the opposite direction.

Pressure   A measure of the amount of a force exerted on an area. In a basketball, the air pressure is about 10 pounds per square inch. For each square inch of surface area, the force exerted by the air is 10 pounds.

Vapor   The gaseous state of a substance that typically exists as a liquid or solid. Water vapor is water in a gaseous state.

Vulcanization   A process, discovered by Charles Goodyear, of strengthening rubber that made it usable in a wide variety of products. Goodyear turned a laboratory accident into his life's crowning achievement when heating a mixture of rubber and sulfur. He named the process after the Roman god of fire, Vulcan.

Art Credits

All artwork courtesy of or by the author except as noted below:

Photo courtesy AIP Emilio Segrè Visual Archives, Brittle Books Collection: page 30

Photo courtesy The Conestoga Company: page 91

Photos by Howard W. Fisher: pages 26 (both), 90

Photos courtesy National Aeronautics and Space Administration: pages 2, 5, 12 (both), 13, 37, 38 (top), 41, 67

Photo courtesy PD Photo.org: page 34

Photo by Adrian Pingstone, courtesy Wikipedia.com: page 89

Photo by Pam Roth, courtesy Wikipedia.com: page 31

Illustration by Gary Smith, Performance Design: title page

Photos courtesy U.S. National Oceanic and Atmospheric Administration: pages 20, 36, 38 (bottom)

Photo by Rini Vella: page vi

Photos courtesy Wikipedia.com: pages 15, 28, 86

Cover Artwork:

Photo by pocheco, a.k.a Sarah Dawn Nichols, courtesy stock.XCHNG: front cover, hot-air balloon (upper left)

Photo by datarec, a.k.a Grzegorz Niewiandomski, courtesy stock.XCHNG: back cover, hot-air balloon (upper right)

Illustrations by Gary Smith, Performance Design: front cover, rocket (center) and bottle rocket car (lower right)

Photo by Rini Vella: back cover, Ed Sobey and students (lower left)

Index